Weight Loss Scripts

WWW.KEY-HYPNOSIS.COM

David Mason © 2013
Version 6

Contents

WEIGHT LOSS SCRIPTS   3
Virtual Gastric Band   6
Emotional Eating   20
Eating Habits Anchoring Script   29
Six Step Reframe Weight Loss Script   39
Night Time Weight Loss Script   47
Motivation for Exercise and Diet   50
Change the past   67
Relaxation for Weight Loss   72
Better Eating Habits   81
Stop eating chocolate   89
Emotional Release hypnotherapy   98
Self Hypnosis for weight loss   107

BONUS SCRIPTS   114
Self Confidence Hypnosis Script   114
Write your own future   127
Weight Loss Checklist   135

Weight Loss Scripts

Select the script that most closely matches the issues you are presented with.

Problem	Script
Overeating	Virtual Gastric Band
Emotional Eating	Emotional Eating
Compulsive Eating	Eating Habits Anchoring
Bingeing	Six Step Reframe
Bad eating	Night Time Script
Motivation	Motivation for Exercise and Diet
Moving on	Change the past
No confidence	Relaxation for Weight Loss
Change Habits	Better Eating Habits
Chocolate	Stop eating chocolate
Comfort Eating	Emotional Release hypnotherapy
Always failing	Self Hypnosis for weight loss

Using the scripts

The scripts are arranged into groups according to their main function, but all the scripts are divided into independent sections so that you can mix and match sections from different scripts and cut and paste them to create new scripts for yourself.
This means that you should examine scripts from all areas to find parts that you can adapt when designing a treatment for a particular client.

Most of the scripts are ready to use exactly as they are. Some are edited transcripts of hypnotherapy sessions and show how to go about dealing with type of client, rather than being intended to be used word for word. Every client who comes to your office is unique and therefore you should study the transcripts to understand how the problem was tackled, and then take sections and adapt these for your own use.

Some scripts are not traditional hypnotherapy scripts but are in the form of metaphor stories. These usually inserted into a regular hypnotherapy session to give the therapy a broader application.

Effective Suggestions
Key Hypnosis Scripts consist of suggestions intended to change behaviors. Everyone has beliefs about who they are, what they can do and how the world works. Everyone has stored behaviors that they automatically apply in specific situations. It is when these inner beliefs and automatic reactions no longer fit the client's outer world that problems arise. Therefore every hypnotic suggestion needs to be aimed at a specific aspect of the client's inner beliefs about the world or at a specific aspect of unconscious behavior.

Hypnotic suggestions will work when they are
a) targeted precisely at one of the client's beliefs or behaviors, and
b) use a technique that matches how the mind functions.

Hypnotic suggestions that do not do both these things will be ignored by the unconscious mind.

Structure of a suggestion

To create an effective suggestion, the therapist needs to decide
a) what behavior is causing the problem,
b) what belief is linked to the behavior,
c) what hypnotic technique to use to cause the change, and
d) how to word the suggestion - Direct, Indirect, Metaphor, etc.

Key Scripts use a logical way of showing how each line of the script works.
Each script is laid out in four columns.

Target	Suggestion	Logic	Comment

The first column identifies the target belief to be changed, or the part of the behavior cycle that is being addressed. The second column holds the wording of the suggestion, what is actually said to the client.

Sometimes the suggestion signals which part of the wording is making the change, in some suggestions it should be obvious and is not shown specifically.

The third column has a shorthand code to show what modality (representation system) is being aimed at, or the hypnotic logic that is being used.

A	Auditory target	encouraging an auditory recall
D	Direct Suggestion	Explicit instruction
I	Indirect Suggestion	Implied instruction
K	Kinesthetic target	aiming at a muscular memory reaction
M	Metaphor	to engage indirect associations
V	Visualization	to implant an image
/	Opposite	The more of one thing the less of the other thing
=	Equivalence	One thing is the same as another thing
>	Cause and Effect	Doing one thing causes the other thing

The fourth column has comments further explaining what perhaps several lines are doing, or specifying the main target of the hypnotic effect.

Using these guides you should be able to follow the logic of the scripts. Once you understand the logic of how a script or technique works you can then use that as the basis for your own original wording and ideas.

Good luck with your clients and I hope these scripts allow you to open up your talents and suggest ways for you to become ever more effective.

Dave Mason

Virtual Gastric Band

Surgery for weight loss involves tying a band around the stomach to reduce its capacity so that stomach cannot hold a lot. This Virtual Gastric Band script uses hypnosis to convince the unconscious mind that a gastric band has been fitted. The script starts with suggestions of going to a hospital and feeling the band being fitted. It is then suggested that with the hypnotic band in place you will feel full with just a mouthful of food.

The Virtual Gastric Band script is an effective hypnotherapy for weight loss. The script includes sections on being confident around food, parts therapy for weight loss, forgiveness of the past, ego strengthening and hypnotic visualization of weight loss.

Target	Induction section		Comment
	Before you begin going into your hypnotic trance now just make yourself comfortable. Just settle yourself down and you can relax now. All you have to do is to focus on becoming comfortable.	D	Bind
	Take a moment now and wiggle about until you are in the right position for what comes next.	I	lack of Reference
	Look around your body and notice if there is any tightness, or any discomfort, and maybe just shrug everything until you are happily settled down and ready. If anything is making you uncomfortable then fix it.		
	Fixing things stops them bothering you doesn't it?		Truism
	Now, in a moment I am going to get you to count down from ten to one, and when you get to one you will have relaxed into a deep satisfying trance. But before that you can move every part of your body as you become loose and floppy and relaxed.		Bind
	Now take a deep breath and relax it. Just let		Progressive

	it all flow out... ahhhhh. That's right. Now tense up your whole body, and then let go again... really relax... and feel how good that is...	relaxation induction
	TEN... focus your attention on your feet ... think about your feet... think about letting your feet and toes and ankles relax and get loose.	
	NINE... Now relax all the muscles in your legs... in you calves, your knees your thighs ... very relaxed... feel those legs getting heavy and heavier...	
	EIGHT... now feel that relaxation spreading into your body... your chest...	
	SEVEN... and now feel that relaxation in your shoulders... spreading all the way down your arms... down to your hands... your fingers... and those arms feel so heavy... so relaxed... it is as if they belong to someone else...	
	SIX... and now allow your neck to relax... and become aware of your face relaxing... your cheeks... your jaw... your lips ...	
	FIVE... let your eyes relax... your eyebrows ... your forehead...	
	FOUR... and everything feels loose and heavy... as if your arms and legs were made of stone... totally relaxed... you can feel the weight pressing down... and you just can't move those arms and legs now... and you can enjoy this feeling of total relaxation... letting go... and the more you relax the more you can relax...	
	THREE... and as your mind drifts off you feel a wave of relaxation traveling down your body ... down and down... from the top of your head... relaxing your face... relaxing	

	your neck... your shoulders your body... spreading... down and down... gently and easily... feel your body sinking down... safe and warm and secure...		
	TWO... and each soft gentle breath out... is relaxing you more... and that relaxing means you can relax deeper and deeper now... letting go... drifting away... nothing matters... enjoying that that lovely feeling...		
	ONE... and totally relaxed now... totally at ease... and your mind can drift away to a place... far, far away... a place where you feel relaxed... where you feel comfortable... always... and think of what the place is like... what other places there might be that you make you feel comfortable... maybe a beach at twilight... or a favorite chair... or snuggled warm in bed on a stormy night... or maybe floating in warm water... allow your mind to drift over these things and other things... whatever feels right for you... as you drift ever deeper... enjoying the feeling ... nothing matters... nothing is important... just being in the moment... let your mind empty...		Dissociation
	Virtual gastric binding operation section		
	and you find yourself lying on trolley... in a corridor somewhere... and there is a cloth draped over you... you are warm and comfortable... dreamy and dozy... completely relaxed... and you can smell the clean smell of antiseptics... and crisp fresh linen...	V	
	and you know that today you are going to be changed... that when you wake up you will be different... you will feel different... you will be starting a new life...	D	Priming
	and there are figures in green around you...	V	

	and you feel a hand on your wrist briefly... and then people by the sides of the trolley you are lying on... and you feel it moving... and you are vaguely aware of noises around you... and the ceiling lights going by... and the sensation of rolling...		
	and as you are being pushed along... each passing object makes you more disoriented... you begin to feel yourself slipping ever deeper... and everything become quiet and calm... and a sense of expectation growing in you...	>	
	and then you sense being in room ... with a big light above... but you don't care... nothing seems to matter to you... you are relaxed and drifting and happy that finally it is being done...	I	
	and somehow you sense something happening on your tummy... you feel something being spread on your skin... skilled hands are doing something... and a sensation of pressure... and you can sense rather than feel that something is happening inside you...	K	
	and at the same time... part of your mind is free to drift up to the ceiling... and you can see yourself... see the incision... see deep inside yourself... all the organs of your body... and there is the pipe that takes food into your stomach...	V	
	and as you watch... a rubbery elastic band is fitted around that pipe... a simple operation... and it is over so quickly... and it seems so small... and you wonder how food will ever get through that... but you know that it has all been planned with the greatest care... you feel it being tested and checked...		

	and there is a feeling of satisfaction in the room... a job well done... carefully you are closed up again... and everyone relaxes...		
	and you are relaxing... it's all over... that band is fitted now...		
	Personal Strength Section		
	you can visualize that band... pinched around the entrance to your stomach... strong and secure... protecting you...safe and strong... imagine every part of it... feel it there... ready to work...	V	
	and knowing that band is there means that you are protected now...	=	
	every time you feel that band in place you know that means that all those old feelings are fading...	=	
Capability	You know that that band means that you are free now... free to live the life you want... the life you deserve...		
Behavior	allowing that band to be put there means that you have taken a major step towards your new way of living... towards your new life...		
	Photo Album Section		
	and I wonder if you can imagine being outside a room somewhere... the kind of room that gets filled with stuff that people can't throw away, but don't have any use for...	M	Old stuff collected and stored
	and you can go into that room... safe and secure...		Safety
	and in that room there is a book... a big book...	M	r
Capability	and you can open that book... and it's a kind of photo album... but this album is special... this album contains every important event		Metaphor

	in your life... but it is more than that... it is a multi-media album... there are pictures and sounds and videos... in there is everything you have done... everything you said... everything ever said to you that affected you... hurt you... made you feel bad... everything you have seen... everything that was done to you... it's all there...	
Capability	But this is the book of your mind... and in this state... now... at this time... you can change things in your mind... you can change what you remember... what happened... what was said... what was done to you... what you lived through...	D
Capability	no matter what happened... you can change it now... having that band in place means that you are now able to think about things differently...	D
Memory	you can go through that book... and you can choose anywhere to start... open the book at say... age 22... see how you looked... how you felt then... and then going backwards... age 20... 18... 16... when you were a teenager... 14... 12... a teenager at school... remember that time... how you were... how you felt... and 10 and 8 and 6... a little child... and before then...	Regression
Capability	and you have the power to change things now... the right to change them...	D
	You can go through that book... and there are pictures... memories... of things that happened... and anything you don't like... anything that hurt you... well, you can rip it out... you can pull that picture out of the book and destroy it... totally... and anything that was said to you... you can just erase it... wipe it out like it never happened... and wipe out the memory of when it was said...	

	and who said it... and anything that happened... you can go back and make it turn out the way it should have... the way you prefer it ... the way you deserve it to have happened... and you can go back now... and think through what happened.. and change it... make it come out the way you want it to... the way that suits you... the way that puts you on top... makes you feel good...	
Capability	Because you have the right and the ability and the permission to change those things...	D
Capability	You can go through that album now... changing... deleting... making right...	M
	and see yourself... at age 5... how you were, what you were like... and then 7 and 9... growing up... and you can remove any pages that you don't like... just throw them away... they can't affect you any more... and anything that happened you can remember it differently... the way it should have been... and that old stuff can just fade away now... and 11 and 13 becoming a teenager... all the stuff that happened then... you can choose to delete it... wipe it away... and 15 becoming a young adult ... and 17 ... and 19 and 21 ... and after that ... remember all those things... and enjoy that freedom to wipe away old stuff...	V
Behavior	and over the next hours and days and weeks you mind can keep on changing those things... getting rid of old feelings... old ideas... old hurts... that were holding you back...	D
Memory	And you can remember all the good times... there were good times too... and you can take a few moments now to go over those good times... and see them... experience	V

	them in bright colors... happy sounds... large and fresh... let the feeling of that happiness fill you now...	
Behavior	and you can take that book... filled with happy images... with good memories... and take it with you... out of that room... leaving all that old stuff behind...	M
	come away from that room... with that book... and then close the door behind you... and lock it... leave all that old stuff where it belongs...	M
Memory	and as you walk away from there... that room begins to fade... and all the stuff in it... and soon that room has disappeared and there is nothing left of it...	V
Capability	and you are free to enjoy those good memories... to look forward now... and everything is brighter for you...	I
Capability	You can now be what you want to be...	D
	Kinesthetic metaphor pattern interrupt	
	and you are becoming aware of your own body... of changes to it... and you can feel something different in your stomach... there is a tightness there...	
	and focus your attention now on your stomach... on that place... where the operation was done...	K
	now imagine your stomach... think of how you used to feel when you knew you had over eaten...when you felt guilt or regret or bad in some way... that feeling you know so well... that familiar feeling... get that feeling how... remember how it used to be to have that feeling...	K
	Do you have that feeling? Are you feeling that feeling?	

	[await an answer... if the client doesn't have the feeling move on to the next section]		
	[if yes] now imagine the feeling in your tummy... in whatever way makes sense to you... and imagine that feeling beginning to spin... to turn...	V	Anchor to a physical feeling
	allow it to turn and remember that bad feeling... but then think about the gastric band inside you now...	K	
	and as you think about that band... and its power to interrupt... to stop you over eating... think about that spinning sensation... and imagine it becoming different... imagine that smooth familiar flow stopping or shrinking or turning the other way...	V	pattern interrupt
	feel that old feeling getting broken up... and losing its power... as new feelings take over... new feelings of confidence...	D	replace pattern
	Direct Suggestion section		
Perception	And from now on the smallest bit of food feels huge... you feel full with a just a mouthful or two...	D	
Perception	your stomach feels full all the time... you get sick at the thought of a too full stomach...	D	
Behavior	Food no longer interests you much... when you think of food... you think of fruit and vegetables... of eating lightly... delicately... delicious natural foods...	D	
	And you are more and more getting good eating habits...	D	
Behavior	Now you look forward to being hungry... being hungry means that you are eating properly... that it is working... that you are improving... that things are the way they should be...	=	Reframing

Rule	only eating at when you are hungry... genuinely hungry... and you are really good at feeling the difference between anxiety and hunger...	D	
Rule	eating only at meal times... the idea of eating anywhere but at a table disturbs you...	D	
Rule	from on... you don't ever eat out of a tin or packet or pot... you only eat a measured amount... away from where it is made or available... and you only ever eat from small container, a little bowl or plate...	D	
Perception	the idea of putting fatty foods into your mouth revolts you... you can taste the grease coating your teeth... your tongue... and it just makes you want to spew...	D	Aversion
Rule	and after you eat from the bowl or plate... you put the empty container away... and wait twenty minutes... and you enjoy finding that you don't need any more...	D	
Rules	And you enjoy making rules... no eating anything with added sugar... no eating anything with more than ten percent fat...	D	
Perception	you don't even notice cakes and pies and sugary foods... the thought of chocolate is off putting...when you think about it... it's really just a mixture of congealed fat and sugar	D	
Perception	and anything sugary in your mouth gives you revolting taste... it would be like putting road kill in your mouth... all maggots and flies and disease... you just don't like sweet things any more...	K	Post Hypnotic Suggestion
Behavior	but you can look forward eating properly now...enjoying healthy natural food... properly cooked, properly prepared... eaten slowly and enjoyed... you are now free to enjoy eating... you can enjoy cooking or		

	dining... knowing you are eating yourself well... and knowing that can let your relax now... deeper and deeper relaxed... as you think of how good your life will be...		
	Capability: you can change		
Capability	and as you are relaxing there now... eyes closed... breathing gently... you may not realize it... but you are changing ...	D	non sequitur
Capability	you are becoming more resourceful... more sure of yourself... more aware of your own ability to change...	D	
Identity	You think about yourself differently now...	D	
Capability	You know that you can change... you can feel yourself changing...you can feel that band round your stomach.	D	
Capability	and this means you can change your habits... easily and quickly... you know you can do this... with a bit of help... and this is exactly the help you need...	>	
Rule	the way you think affects your behavior... what you do... what you can do... what you find easy to do...		Truism
Behavior	And there is one thing you are going to do... You are going to eat properly from now on...	D	
Identity	You are going to end those old eating habits today... you are never going to eat unless you are really hungry...	D	
	You are in control		
Capability	Because you are getting more and more control in every part of your life now...	>	Non sequitur
behavior	You are becoming aware now of how much control you have... and having that control means you have less and less anxiety in stressful situations...	>	
Capability	You can deal with anxiety... and with any problems that come up in your day...	> D	

Behavior	And because of that you are more determined... more convinced... more sure that what you feel in your stomach now has changed you forever...	
RULE	There are no safe snacks... every extra nibble is a danger... everything you don't need is just extra weight... there is no 'just a taste, just one bit"... ever... for you... any more...	
Behavior	If you ever get too close to uncontrolled eating you will feel an irresistible compulsion to get up and leave... you will start walking away... find yourself somewhere safe... away from it... and you mind will be filled with alarm bells ... You will take deep breaths until the danger is over and you are flooded with relief and calm again...	Post Hypnotic Suggestion
Behavior	you don't need to use food for emotions any more... you are done with that...	D
	and when friends say 'oh have one more... just a bit won't hurt'... a feeling rises up in you... and you feel an irresistible urge to push it away...	
	when you see ads for food you see through them... you now see the reality... that it puts on weight... it is killing people for money... and you reject it all...	
	Change the part that wants to eat	
Identity	There is a part of you that wanted to eat... a familiar part... You may not know that part but it is there... and it is ready to change... now... at a deep level you know it is time to change... to let go... that part had a good reason to eat... but things have changed now...	
Capability	Tell that part that it is now to change... thank that part for what it was trying to do... but it	

17

	is time to change now... every part of you is valuable... so you can convert that part to do something else... that part of you that used to want to want to eat to make you feel better is now being converted to a useful healthy purpose...	
Identity	And that part of you will be glad... and it is changing now because you asked it to... and you can be surprised at how effective that change can be... and how you are different now...	ambiguity
	Visualization Section	
	Allow your mind to drift away... to a few months from now... and you are walking along by some shops... and you are looking in fashion shops... shoe shops... enjoying window shopping...	
	and in the window you catch sight of a woman looking straight at you... and she is beautifully dressed... slim and elegant... poised and confident...	
	and you look back at her... and then you realize that you are looking at your reflection...	
	and that is your ideal self... at your ideal weight...	
	and she looks at you... with an expression on her face... and she is encouraging you... and somehow you know what she did to make it all happen...	
	and you are aware of how good she feels... how confident she is... and that confidence spreads to you...	
	Reorientation	
	And when you have done that you will come back to the present... knowing that something wonderful has happened... and	

	you are back in charge of your life.	
	So begin counting now from five up to one… quietly to yourself… and when you get to one… you will be back in the present… fully alert… ready to start on that new life of yours…	

Emotional Eating

This script is aimed at the person who knows that they shouldn't eat but gives in to temptation every time. It focuses on stopping eating sugar, but can be adapted to other things. It works to convince the client that being in hypnosis gives them a special ability to change, and then builds on the theme of change to help them stop their problem eating. The suggestions include replacing dieting with a life style change, and gives simple rules to follow to lose weight. It also addresses the issues of emotional eating due to moods.

	Induction		
	Allow yourself to relax now... as you start to go into trance take a deep breath and then let it go... and another...		bind
	And as you are lying there... breathing gently... relaxing in that chair... become aware that each breath is making your arms and legs heavy ... heavy and tired.		Breathing induction
	And as you think about that tiredness...as you feel your body responding ... your eyes are beginning to get heavy now... heavy and tired... and as you feel that tiredness, heaviness growing those eyes can relax too... relax completely...	K	Said slowly with the breathing
	And that lets you feel even more relaxed... going deeper and deeper ... with every breath out... deeper and deeper... more and more relaxed...	K	Pace with breathing
	And as you hear these words... making you more at ease... everything around you can fade away... and every sound, every word, is taking you deeper and deeper...		
	You don't have to do anything... you don't have to listen... you don't have to think... all you have to do is to enjoy that wonderful feeling of deep deep relaxation... as the		

		sound of my voice guides you to another place...		
	Belief in the power of Hypnosis			
Belief	You are getting ready for a new start, a better way of living, a healthy way of living... to have the life you want... a way to get what you really want...	D	Ambiguity to cover all possibilities
Capability	By coming here today, you have started on the road to having the body you want... to becoming who you want to be... to being your ideal body weight...	D	Reason for change
Capability	By choosing hypnosis you are going to be able to open up all the powers of your own mind... and to use those powers to change how you feel and act and think...	>	Need...
Belief	Hypnosis changes every part of your mind... so you can change every part of your body... and that means you can get control over your body by changing your behavior...	>	... method.
Capability	And that will give you the ability to get the shape and weight you want... easily and forever...		...result...
Belief	...problem eating will be a thing of the past.	D	... outcome
	Change is happening now		
Capability	What you are doing now will ensure that you can change permanently	>	Ambiguity
	Your subconscious mind needs to change...		Need...
	...and this session today will make those changes ...		... method...
	... and change at the center changes every part of every cell throughout your whole body...		... result...
Capability	...which means that every cell is now filled with power...		...outcome
Behavior	... the power that will carry you on to		

21

	success.		
	Banish Dieting		
Rule	Losing weight is a success. Eating better is a success. Clever weight loss is about managing your eating. Eating is a pleasure... dieting is a drag... you don't have to diet to lose weight...	D	Need
Behavior	You won't have to diet any more... diet is about denial... about ignoring your body...		Need
Behavior	dieting doesn't work... hypnosis does... you will succeed with hypnosis.	>	Resource
Identity	Hypnosis will enable you to let the weight go...	D	Method
Behavior	... through hypnosis you will be able to eat a little and feel full...	>	Result
Behavior	with hypnosis you respond to your own needs...		resource
	you acknowledge your body... you allow yourself to feel comfortable and free...		method
Capability	so you won't ever fail again... failure is now in the past	D	result
Behavior	And looking back on it, you will be surprised at how easy it all was... that you didn't need willpower or anything else...	D	Dissociation
	... with hypnosis you just don't feel like eating ...	D	
	Stop Emotional eating		
Behavior	And because you have changed... from now on you are becoming more aware of the signals you get from your stomach... how your stomach communicates about hunger.		Monitor feelings
Behavior	Every time you think you feel hungry... you pause and think about what your stomach is telling you...		
Rule	Your stomach might signal anxiety as well		Reframe

22

	as hunger...		
Capability	... you can learn to tell the difference...		Resource
	When you notice that your stomach is trying to say something...		Method
Behavior	when you notice a feeling in your stomach... you carefully check on what the message is...		method
Behavior	before you take food from the fridge... before you raise food or drink to your mouth... you check if you are actually hungry... or if it is something else...		Method
	...is it hunger or is it actually nerves?		Reframe
	and if the result is that you are not feeling genuine hunger... then you put the food away...		
	you listen to your body now... you take care of your body now... and if you don't need to eat, then you don't eat...		
	And that makes you feel better...		Outcome
	Metaphor for metabolism		
	And feeling better lets you manage your own eating...	>	
Memory	I wonder if you can remember what it was like to be on a swing... maybe in a park or a garden somewhere...	K	Metaphor of control
	And sitting in that swing you can move your body to make the swing go higher and higher... safely enjoying the power to move...	M	Demonstrate control
	Or you can let the swing slow down now... and imagine swinging gently back and forth...		Can slow down
	And feeling the feeling of that swing... as that swing slows down... each movement soothes you... calms you... and you can allow each movement to take you deeper		Deepener

23

	and more relaxed...		
Capability	When you are on that swing... you have control over how fast it goes, or how slow... you can decide how high or how low... and you can decide whether you even want to swing at all...		Reminder of own ability
Capability	So you have control over what you want to have happen	D	Affirmation
Capability	And you can control your own internal swings... you can become aware of mood swings... and being aware... you can just accept them and then choose either to go on up... or to slow down...	D	Control swings
	It's the same with eating... you can choose what level of activity you want your body to work at... its metabolism...	I	Control metabolism
	Your mind controls your body... and after hypnosis you can control your mind...	I	Resource
	... so you can get your mind to adjust your metabolism... to a safe level... a level that lets you burn off the food you eat...	>	
	and your body will adjust your intake to match your level of activity.	D	
	so that you eat just enough... and your body adjusts to just the right weight for you...	D	
	... automatically... easily... up and down... to exactly meet your needs...	D	
	... to the point that you don't even think about food any more... you eat when you are hungry... and don't when you are not... automatic, effortless... normal eating to maintain a healthy size...	D	
	Aversion to sugar		
	And thinking about what you want to have... take a deep breath now... breathe in deeply and relax... with each breath you are	K	Deepener

	relaxing more and more...		
Memory	and as you are relaxing... think about what you like to eat... think about the things you enjoy most...		
	And as you think about food, you realize that because the hypnosis has opened up your mind... you are seeing it differently...	>	Reframe
Behavior	From now on you are becoming more aware of what your body needs... your body needs food... but it needs only the right food...		Reframe
Behavior	You now realize that some foods are just not for you... as your mind is changing so your tastes are changing...	D	
	every time you feel sugar in your mouth you feel it coating your teeth... like thick grease building up in your mouth... and that feeling increases until you feel you must brush your teeth to get rid of that horrible film on your teeth...	K	Texture
	The taste of sugary sweet things makes you want to gag...	D	Taste
	Every time you see a soda bottle you imagine some horrible living thing like worms inside... something disgusting... and you have no desire to let that into your stomach...		Sodas
	Cookies and cakes remind you of the hidden sugar and grease... the idea of putting that mix of unhealthy gritty greasy stuff in your mouth is disgusting to you now... it would be like putting some revolting dead thing into your mouth...		Cookies
	Crunching on a cookie you can imagine your teeth cracking and collapsing...		
	The thought of that sugar flowing around your veins... slowing and clogging your		

	blood... damaging your health ... makes you wary of sugar in all its forms...		
Behavior	You find now that instead of sweet things, you prefer savory. The taste of cinnamon and other spices now appeal to you instead.		prefer
Behavior	you just don't like sugar anymore.	D	
	5 simple rules		
	Repeat these rules in your mind until they are part of you... these simple rules will change how you succeed...		
	From now on I am taking control of my eating		
Rule	I don't eat within an hour of finishing eating...		
Rule	I wait for twenty minutes before deciding if I need more...		
Rule	I never eat within three hours of bed time...		
Rule	I won't eat anything that tastes greasy...		
Rule	Half of every meal will be green...		
Rule	There will no more excuses, no jokes, no exceptions, about eating fattening foods...		
	I pause in eating as soon as I have eaten half the food... before my stomach actually feels full.	D	
	That's right... so take a deep breath now... and allow your mind to clear		New topic
	Feeling bad does not equal eating		
	And there will be some days when you don't do so well... and that's OK too.	D	Reframe
Capability	Now that you have started on the change... you will recognize these things for what they are...	D	ambiguity
Situation	There are times when you feel down... when you feel angry perhaps... disappointed... there are many things that happen... that		

	cause you to feel low...		
Behavior	Those things do happen... will happen... so you need to plan for them...		Resource
	you need to say to yourself 'something is affecting my mood... and so I get curious about it... but I don't let it get to me...'		Method
Rule	'feelings have nothing to do with food'	D	Affirmation
	'feelings have nothing to do with food'	D	repeat
Identity	'I don't let my feelings affect who I am... the feelings will pass... and I will succeed'	D	Outcome
Behavior	And even if I do eat stupidly once, that is OK, because I have a plan, not a diet... I have a life style... not a fad...	D	Reframe
Behavior	And that means I can let it go... and keep on healthy eating...	D	Resource
Capability	... and that way I succeed... because it is more than one day... I think in weeks and months now...	D	Method
	... and everything balances out...		Outcome
	Repeat and summarize		
Capability	Because hypnosis has strengthened your mind... you are more in control now...	D	Resource
Capability	...you can control what you eat... so you can lose weight... by eating naturally...	>	Method
Rule	...and by eating naturally you will get the shape you want.	D	Outcome
	Your mind has the power to do what you want	D	Truism
Identity	You are in control now... you can choose how you feel... you see things differently... because you are different...	D	
Rule	As you start to lose weight you will feel hungry. This normal and natural and to be expected. In fact you should look forward to it, because it means that you are eating		Avoid relapse

27

	right...	
	When you are doing it right, you will wake hungry... and you can enjoy that feeling... knowing what it means for you...	Reframe
	And during the day... when you feel hungry... you can rejoice... because that means it is working... you are losing weight... you get comfort from that feeling...	Reframe
	It is sign that you are succeeding... it means that you are eating less... and the next thing you know your clothes will start to be loose on you... and you are now on the way to getting the figure you want to have...	Meaning
	Reorientation	
	And with all those things in mind, when you are ready, you can begin to count from five up to one, quietly to yourself.	
	When you get to one you will be fully awake, alert... and ready to feel different...	
	So begin counting NOW.	

Eating Habits Anchoring Script

This script is intended to be used where a client has an eating problem, can control it sometimes, but then feels compelled to start again.
Part of it is based the technique of anchoring and part on visualization. It links the client's inner strengths and personal beliefs to external triggers, so that when the trigger event happens they are reminded of their inner strengths.

The script uses three different anchoring strategies. One section uses a physical metaphor to anchor feelings of determination to squeezing their fist shut. One section uses the idea of a Magic Word. This is associated to a visual metaphor and is used to remind them that they have the ability to succeed if ever they feel temptation to start again. One section uses the anchor between a color and the desired situation. The script uses a post hypnotic suggestion of using the color to constantly remind them that they can succeed in not doing the eating any more.

	Induction		
	[Make sure the client has their hands free]		
	And it's odd for me to think of you sitting there now... just breathing gently... wondering about... how easily... how quickly... you can go into that lovely relaxed state...	I	Ambiguity -
	and while wondering... maybe you can imagine someone just like you... some other person wanting to go into that relaxed dreamy state... and how you could help that person into that state of comfort... of quiet relaxation... and you might imagine saying to that person... become aware of your breathing... of how your breath moves gently in and out... and tell them... how on every breath out ... you can relax a little		My Friend John induction

	more... and just rest for a few moments... and allow time to relax... deeply... completely... and notice how that relaxation progresses... smoothly...		
	... and then get them to imagine a quiet, peaceful spot... maybe on a warm afternoon... to imagine lying comfortably... somewhere nice... mind drifting away... imagine arms and legs... eyelids... are beginning to feel tired and heavy... as heavy as lead... to relax ... totally... to just let things go... and drift away...		
	...and now imagine being at the top of an escalator... a moving staircase... looking down... and allow them to be carried down that escalator... safely and securely... carried gently down and down... more deeply relaxed... as that escalator goes down.. carried deeper and deeper... the body relaxes more... and your mind relaxes more... going deeper and deeper with every comfortable breath... and by and by you are drifting off into an endless velvety welcoming dreamland...		Deepener
	Therapy section		
Identity	In this session you are going to learn how to use self hypnosis. This will give you the strength you need to get the result you want. You have a natural ability to go into trance anytime you want.	I	You have the ability
Capability	This may not be something you are familiar with, but it is something you can do easily once you have experienced what it is like.	D	
	You already know the difference between tension and relaxation, so you already know the basics of it, don't you?	>	Bind
	You have been able to stop eating at times,		Empathy

	but something seems to be trying get you to think about doing the bad eating behavior again, even though part of you doesn't want to...		
Rule	This is telling you something important...		Reframe
Capability	it is telling you that you need to be able to remind yourself whenever that feeling comes back, of why you need to stop...	D	
	and to remind yourself that you can change... that you have that power... that you can succeed...		Reconnect to success
Capability	With self hypnosis you will succeed in controlling the physical and emotional tension you feel about eating.	>	
Capability	With this skill you will experience things in a new way, a way that gives you the confidence, strength and success you need.	D	Inevitability
Capability	It will help you reduce anxiety because hypnosis is a mental process that leads to physical relaxation and physical relaxation leads to letting go tension... and letting go tension means you can stop the eating need...	>	
Identity	You will feel stronger and more confident.	D	Outcome
	With self hypnosis you will experience your feelings from a new perspective, and this will let you dismiss temptation with confidence and calmness.	>	Reframing
	Clenched fist physical metaphor		
	You are now going to learn how to boost your resistance.		
	While you are in this state of deep relaxation... your breathing is slow and steady... your body is relaxed... every muscle loose and heavy...		Pacing
Identity	This state is something that you have		Leading

	created... on your own... and in your own way... and the way you experience it is unique to you...		
Identity	You have the ability to return to this state any time you want to...	D	Leading
Capability	and when you are in this state you can perform the most amazing things... with the most amazing strengths... because your mind is focused	>	
	it is a state of inner strength... a state that lets you get in touch with higher powers... a state that lets you transcend your normal self... to summon inner resources and create powerful... almost magical effects.	D	Connect to beliefs
Capability	And you have the natural ability to use this special unique state...	D	Ambiguity
	And as you are relaxing there now... breathing gently... you can become aware of your hands... a feeling in your hands... and your mind can select one hand or the other hand... allow your mind to decide... to pick one hand...		Dissociation
	And while most of your body becomes more relaxed you will find that one hand begins to close, to clench into a fist... and then relax again... and as that hand relaxes... you go deeper and deeper inside...		Deepener
	And as you go deeper and deeper inside... you become aware of something... you become aware of something rising up inside you... and you recognize that for what it is... a fierce determination to end the eating habit... a feeling of stubborn refusal to eating the wrong foods at the wrong time...		Reframe physical feeling to mental toughness
	And once again... notice your hand closing... and notice the feeling associated with this... as that hand closes... your mind focuses on		

	why you want to be different now, [mention health, appearance, self-esteem, whatever the client says is motivating her]		
	And that makes you even more aware of what you get from ending that bad behavior... the eating habit... and as you think about that... that feeling of determination... of self-confidence... that you can beat this... that you can stop and change forever... grows ever stronger...		
	And this is where you learn to control that feeling... as that feeling grows... so does your own power... that strength... that determination... that knowledge of how to end it grows... you use that to close your hand into a fist... and that power surges through you ... to an absolute unstoppable power... to succeed... thrust aside all obstacles to reach out and clear away those thoughts... those old ideas that were getting in the way...		
	And as you clench that fist you know that nothing can stand in your way of getting what you want ... you know that it is over for ever... you can beat this... you have beaten this...		
	And as that fist relaxes again... that feeling of triumph... of being unbeatable... fills your mind...		
	And that is what your body has been telling you... that is what you need to learn...		
Behavior	You can get into this comfortable relaxed state anytime... all you need to do is to take three deep breaths... and then relax your muscles... you already know how to do that...		
Capability	And in that state... every time you form that	>	Physical

	hand into a fist you will once again be filled with that feeling of unstoppable confidence... that power surges up in you ... and nothing can stop you... nothing will ever make you eat that way again... .		metaphor
Behavior	In any situation... you will be able to call up that feeling... just by relaxing a little... and close that hand... and that surge of power will be there for you... unstoppable power... power to resist... to succeed... to show you can...	>	
Capability	And as soon as you feel that ... that temptation just fades away... vanishes... like it had never been there...	V	
Capability	And you feel calm and strong and in charge and relaxed... and you can laugh at that temptation... because you have learned how to use your own inner power now...	I	Pre-supposition
Capability	From now on... you know... that anytime you feel that anxiety... or any physical feeling that reminds you of a need to overeat... you can call up that invincible feeling... that sweeps away all those thoughts... by deliberately relaxing the tension in your muscles and then forming that fist... and the tighter you make that fist... the more power you get...	=	Physical metaphor
Capability	And no matter how many times it happened in the past... now that you have learned this simple trick of self-hypnosis... you can walk away... from that temptation... and all those thoughts will seem silly...	>	
Identity	and you can laugh at its attempts to interest you again... that was the old you... you are not interested now and never will be... that is just not who you are any more.		Reframing
	Magic word visualization metaphor		

	And when you look back on those times when you were overeating... you see it in dark colors, like a picture seen far away... dim and obscure... small and faded...	V	
	And think of the first time you felt you needed to eat but didn't want to... see yourself as you were then... and in your mind, rub out the behavior from that picture...		
	And relax... deeper and deeper...		
	And now think about the things you really don't like about that kind of eating ... really focus on them... and allow the feeling of disgust or resentment or whatever word it is that sums up how you feel about compulsive eating... allow yourself to feel that totally... to reject overeating and everything to do with it... think about how much you dislike the feeling of needing to eat... think about how that makes you feel... about yourself ... about what other people think about you...	V	
	And then imagine sweeping away all that bad feeling... imagine you can wipe it out... totally... completely... imagine it as a picture and destroy that picture and you are wiping it out... tear it up, throw it in the rubbish... wipe it clean... paint over it... do whatever you want to do to destroy that picture...	V	Metaphor
Behavior	And you do so, say your power word aloud... you will find the right word... some people say 'strong', some say 'freedom' or use a special made up word or a phrase like 'I am a winner'... 'inner beauty'... whatever seems right to you...	D	
Capability	Just imagine those feelings, those feeling you get when something inside makes you feel	V	Metaphor

	like eating again... and then say your word, and imagine yourself wiping out those feelings... wiping them away like cleaning a worktop... wring it out and flush it away... feel the power of that word... the power that keeps you going... gets you through... makes you feel good about yourself and about your own ability to be strong...		
Behavior	And every time you feel that temptation even starting... at the tiniest hint you think your magic word... and that reminds you of that strength you have... and that image of overeating is destroyed... and you can enjoy vanishing it... mastering it...		
	Magic color post hypnotic suggestion		
	Now take a deep breath... and allow you your mind to drift.		
	Think about a time when you are confident you won't have the old feeling of needing to eat. See yourself in that situation... imagine how it feels, how it looks... what is around you... when you are in the confident state... the state when you know you are in control of your eating and you feel good about that... and you know you won't overeat...	V	
	And now think about another time like that... another situation... when you have that feeling of certainty... that quiet easy feeling that you have your eating under control and you are not even thinking about it...	V	Connect to successes
	Now think about those two situations, those times, and notice what they have in common... what is present in both situations... notice a color that is there in both those situations, and then test it... think of other similar situations... and notice what	V	Connect to more successes

	color is present then...		
Belief	And that color has special significance to you.	D	
Memory	Whenever you think of that color... you will think of those situations when you are confidently in control... and in those situations when see that color... you will immediately feel confident... in control...	>	
Capability	And as you go about the normal things in your day... you will notice that color here and there... and every time you see that color it will bring to mind those feelings of calm... of confident control... and will remind you that you are in control... that you can easily be in control... it will remind you that you can wipe away those images... those symbols... everything associated with the old overeating behavior...	>	
Belief	And really, that can become the color of your life... you can find yourself constantly reminded of your own inner strength... of your success... of how easy it is really...	>	
Behavior	And every time you see that color... it is like you hear a voice in the back of your head saying 'this is easy... I know how to do this... it is working... I am winning... I can forget all about that now... and just ignore it... this is easy...' and you will have succeeded.	A	
	Reinforcing		
	So take a few moments now and enjoy that success to come... allow yourself to settle down and get more comfortable now...		Pacing
Memory	And think over all the things you have experienced in this session... the powers you have awakened... the touch of that inner strength... the feeling of having made contact... the inner knowledge...		ambiguity

Identity	All that means that you have the power to succeed... to sustain the change you are seeking... to be free of eating problems for ever... easily, comfortably... confidently	
Capability	You know how to relax... and that means that in any situation where you need to... you can close your eyes... relax inwardly... and clench that fist... and that will bring back that inner power... the power to free yourself.. to remind yourself of your own strength and ability...	Reinforce FIST
Capability	You now know how to wipe away those feelings... by visualizing the negative images and watching them get destroyed with your power word... you can use that word anytime anywhere to give you power over feelings... to remind you instantly of that determination... to push it away...	Reinforce WORD
Capability	And as you go through your day... that color will remind you of feeling calm and confident... and the constant reminder... looking out for ... noticing... that color... will make you stronger...	Reinforce COLOR
Capability	and you can brush those old feelings away like a stray hair... and forget all about the problem now...	Post hypnotic metaphor
	Reorientation	
	And now... you can count to yourself quietly in your mind... from five up to one... and when you reach one you will be back in the present... fully alert and ready for the rest of your day...	
	So when you are ready... begin counting now.	

Six Step Reframe Weight Loss Script

The Six Step Reframe Script is an NLP technique. The Six Step Reframe for weight loss is used in situations where 'part of me wants to stop bingeing, but part of me enjoys doing it'.

The Reframe technique allows you slow down your thinking so that you can control the different parts of you that are causing your problem.

The Reframe Script is based on Parts Therapy, where one part takes charge and asks other parts to change. The script asks the part that wants to eat to reveal its purpose, and asks it to negotiate with other parts to keep the purpose but change how it does it.

	Induction	
	OK. I want you to understand that you are in control... you are in control at all times... and you can decide exactly how and when you go into trance...	Bind
	Just settle back and make yourself comfortable... Let your arms flop and let your hands relax... maybe shrug your shoulders a little... let your head recline and settle down... jiggle your legs if you want... until things are just the way you want them...	Bodily relaxation
	And now you can take a deep breath... hold that breath ... and as you let it go... allow that breath out to close your eyes...	Eyes closed
	That's good.	Reassure
	And now take another breath... and hold it... and this time as you breathe out... really relax... just become aware of any tension in your muscles... and allow it to relax...	Progressive relaxation
	And when you are ready... take another breath and hold it... and just think about how relaxed you can be... I wonder when was the time you were most relaxed?... I	Transderivational Search

39

	wonder how relaxed it's possible to be?...	
	And you can now let your breathing go back to normal... just focus on your breathing... focus on that gentle movement of air... in ... and out... in... and out....	Pace with breathing
	That's very good... you're doing very well...	Reassure
	and just think about each breath out... feeling more and more relaxed... more at ease... more comfortable... That's right...	
	and with each breath out... you can imagine your own voice in your head... or someone speaking... saying "deeper and deeper"... "more and more"... relaxing...	
	and you can choose how much you want to let go with every breath... and part of your mind can go into trance and while part of your mind can stay alert... and while that part is as alert as you want it to be it can be deciding how deeply you want that other part to go... and let that other part go...	Bind
	and all the while... breathing gently... choosing how deeply to go... continue breathing... relaxing... watching as part of your mind is going deeper... as your inner voice leads you... down and down...	Supposition
	until when you are at right depth for you... allow your mind to choose... one hand or other... and you can be curious as how your mind chooses... one hand instead of the other... as if it is someone else's hand...	Dissociation
	and you'll know when your mind has chosen... you can allow a finger or a thumb or maybe something else to signal that you have reached a comfortable depth... and allow that finger or thumb to move on its own... just let it happen... when it's ready...	Dissociation
	[await signal]	

	Six step reframe - set up the inner place	
	and as you drift around... allow your mind to think of a place... a place in your mind... where you can gather your thoughts and feelings... a place where you can assemble the parts of you that want to change and need to change... a place in your mind where all the parts of you can come out... where they will be safe and welcomed...	
	some people think of a dark cave, some of a large hall, some people imagine a meeting room... allow your mind to find such a place...	
	STEP ONE - Identify the behavior to change	
	Now think about the eating behavior you want to change... think about how you feel when you are in that behavior... think about the part of you that does that behavior... maybe you can visualize it... or feel it... or hear something...	
	Become aware of that part... take your time and think about the part of you that is doing that behavior... take a few slow breaths and let the part come out... allow its presence to get stronger...	
	Now make the part feel welcome... thank the part for coming into awareness... tell the part that you appreciate what it has been trying to do for you... tell it that you really like that part... that you realize it has been trying to help you all this time... working 24/7 to do something positive for you...	
	Really communicate your gratitude... because every part of you is valuable... let it know... in any way that makes sense to you... that you know that its intention was good...	

	STEP TWO - *Communicate with the part*	
	Now ask the part... respectfully... if it is willing to communicate with you...	
	Simply form a question... a feeling... an expectation in your mind... allow that feeling... that need... that expectation to form... to continue... just be aware of that asking...	
	ask the part to let you know that it is willing to communicate... (it may take a while)... ask the part to choose what way it wants to communicate with you... it might be a need to lift a finger, it might be a warmth on your skin... it might be a tingle in your hand... leave it up to the part and scan around your body... until you feel something...	
	Then ask the part to signal again... to repeat the signal... so you know that you have recognized its response... Or you may just get a feeling... a certainty that the part it listening and answering...	
	Thank the part for allowing you to communicate with it... focus on the part... and allow it make itself known even more clearly...	
	STEP THREE - *Identify the part's intention*	
	Now ask the part if it will let you know what its function is... what it is trying to do for you... every part of you is trying to protect you... trying to help you... ask it to let you know what it trying to do, what it thinks it has been aiming for all this time...	
	Now wait... allow the part to make you aware of its intentions... you may get a memory... you may get an image or a symbol or a word... the part will signal in a way that makes sense to it... it will find a	

	way to communicate its purpose to you...		
	When you get the message... it may be obvious... it may be unclear... it may be that somehow you just know what it is about... thank that part for allowing you to share in that knowledge...		
	Allow it to become clear in your mind what the part was trying to do... or find something that symbolizes the intention... or a feeling that sums it up...		
	Now that you know what the part was trying to do for you... tell the part that you appreciate its help... that you recognize its intention was worthwhile... and ask if it is OK if it can still do that for you... but in a different way?		
	Wait for the answer... if you get a clear answer 'yes' or you feel it OK for the change to happen then go on ...		
	if the answer is 'no' then ask the part if it will let you know why it won't change the way it does it... and communicate with the part until it is happy to go on...		
	STEP FOUR - Think about alternatives		
	Now it is time to bring some other parts into that place... and you might think of it as a committee room of some sort... or a convention... a market place... some place where many different parts can come together to meet and mingle...		
	there is a part of you that is creative, that can solve problems... there is a part of you that can manage things... that knows how to put things together... how organize and combine and make the best choices... safely and carefully...		
	there are many parts of you... now ask the		

creative part of you to contact all the other parts... any part that has something to give to help make the change...

and that creative part of you can begin to come up with different ways of getting what the part of you that wanted to eat was trying to do... there are many other ways to achieve... many ways of giving you the positive outcome you need... without having the eating problem as a result...

and the clever part of you can work with that creative part... and get all the other parts to contribute something... and they can all work together to find different ways of getting that outcome... and you can be curious as to how many different ways there are... easy ways... clever ways... safe ways...

and allow all those parts to work together to create those ways for you to consider... and for that part that was making you eat to consider...

STEP FIVE - Choose alternative behavior

become aware of all those ways that are being found... ways of behaving... ways of being... that will give you the outcome to keep you safe, to protect you... the same as you were getting from the part that wanted you to eat...

and now allow your mind to drift... think of all the possible behaviors you could have... all the different ways that the parts created for you to consider... think over what seems to you to be the best... the way to still be safe and protected... but without the eating...

and allow the right answer to come up... on its own... something that seems just right... that you can imagine doing in all those

	situations when you used to eat... decide on the right new behavior... that will let you be in the same situation and not feel the need to eat...	
	STEP SIX - *check for any conflicts*	
	and in that place... with all those parts... now offer up the way you have chosen... for them to consider... get the organizing part to contact all the other parts... get each part... each of the many parts of you that are all... in their own way... protecting you... and want only the best for you... get the organizing part to check that all those other parts are happy with the way you have chosen...	
	that it does not clash with anything they want to do... that would prevent them from doing their care for you...	
	and that organizing part can negotiate and check and be satisfied that every part supports your new way... your new behavior in that old situation...	
	and when all the parts are in agreement... you can ask the original part... the part that was making you eat... if it is satisfied... if it can now change to new way... and still care for you in that old way...	
	and ask it to signal to you...	
	and when it has signaled to you... you can send a message of gratitude to it... thanking it for looking after you for so long... and it can continue its job of looking after you now... in a different way...	
Capability	that old eating behavior can now fade away... to just a memory... and that can fade too...	
	and those parts are changed forever... and	

	that's something else to glad about...	
	as you begin to return to the present...	
	Reorientation	
	And so before coming back to full awareness...	
	take whatever time you need now... to consider those ideas... to allow your mind to examine things from every aspect... like a jeweler looking into the heart of a diamond...	
	and the lessons and possibilities... consider them deeply... absorb them deeply... into your very being... thinking about how best to apply them...	bind: best
	And when you have had enough time to process and learn from this session... then it is time to bring this session to a close..	bind: time
	and you can start coming back to the present... at whatever rate is right for you.	
	...so when you are fully prepared to... you can find yourself back in full awareness of the room around you, feeling refreshed... and knowing that you have finally settled something important.	

Night Time Weight Loss Script

This is a little weight loss script that you can use for a bit of guerrilla hypnosis, like street hypnosis, only you do it in bed, not in the street. You can use this script to help your partner stop over eating, snacking and eating the wrong foods. Use it with your partner as they settle down to sleep.

It is very simple hypnosis, but very effective. It uses direct suggestion just as your partner is drifting off to sleep and implants the suggestion that they will stop bad eating immediately and no longer want to eat outside of meal times.

	The Set up		
	[You and your partner should be lying in bed, ready to go to sleep.]		
	[Start stroking your partner's back, gently drawing your fingers down the back from the shoulders and then continue the light touches until trance is achieved.]	K	Kinesthetic induction
	Weight Loss Induction		
	As you feel those little touches you can feel yourself settling down... settling deeper with each soft stroke... each stroke is relaxing you more and more... and as you relax... your breathing is getting more even... each breath out more and more relaxing...	>	stroking = going deeper
	and feel yourself settling down now... getting more comfortable... feeling warm and safe and cozy... and really relaxing, letting go now...	K	self induction
	focus on your breathing... each breath letting your muscles relax... your arms are relaxing... your legs are relaxing... your whole body is relaxing now...	K	Muscle relaxation
	and allow that to continue as each stroke soothes and softens... gently, softly, leading		

	you deeper and deeper ...		
	[continue stroking until you hear their breathing slow down]		
	Weight Loss Suggestions		
	and as you are relaxing there... breathing softly... feeling the soft touch on your skin... you can notice something changing... something deep inside is altering how you feel...		Ambiguity
	and you can think about tomorrow... about what you will be doing tomorrow...	V	
	and think about how and when you are eating tomorrow...	V	
Behavior	and tomorrow will be different...	D	
Behavior	tomorrow you find your habits changing... you lose all interest in eating between meals... you forget about eating... you have your breakfast... your lunch...	D	
Behavior	and in between you forget all about food...		Amnesia
Behavior	tomorrow you will find that you have no interest in snacks and nibbles... you will find that when you take the first bite of a snack into your mouth... the food tastes like rubber... like some greasy lump... every bite you take tastes strange... a strange unpleasant feeling in your mouth just at the idea of it...	D	Aversion therapy
Behavior	The idea of eating outside of meal times makes you feel queasy... there is a feeling of wrongness about it... you push it out of you mind...	D	
Behavior	and when you think about eating outside of proper meals you get a taste in your mouth like rubber... or like chewing sand... dirt...	D	
Behavior	and from now on you enjoy your meals... healthy meals... meals you eat slowly and		

	appreciate... meals eaten at the right time and the right place... you really like having a good healthy meal...	
Behavior	and between meals the idea of eating is disgusting... all wrong... just thinking about it makes you turn away...	
	and thinking about it now... you are thinking about how you will enjoy your regular meals... eating the right food... at the right time...	
	and nothing else... nothing interests you any more about snacking... extra food just makes you feel bad... and it so good to just forget about it... like it was never there...	Amnesia
	Termination	
Capability	and you can feel really good about that... feel good about yourself... and thinking about feeling good... about good eating... good living... good health...	
	you can feel yourself going into a good sleep... a deep sleep... refreshing sleep... all night...	
Behavior	until tomorrow... when it is all different... a new day and a new feeling... towards a new life... Sleep well now...	

Motivation for Exercise and Diet

This script is for anyone who needs to be motivated to get out and exercise, and to eat a healthier diet. It mixes direct hypnotic suggestions with metaphors for self esteem, leaving behind bad influences, changing inner beliefs and taking charge of your life. The script is in several sections. You do not need to use all the sections at once. Only use the sections that you think are most appropriate for this particular client.

	Induction		
	Are you sitting comfortably? Ready to begin? That's good		Yes set
	Just raise your toes up. Put your hands out like that... and put your head back.		
	That's good... now I'd like you to take a deep breath and hold it, and just *haaaaa*... let it go... that's good...	I	Relax the body
	now take another breath and this time as you breathe out just allow those tired eyes to close... that's good...	I	close the eyes
	and now another breath... and just allow your head to assume a comfortable position... that's good...	I	drop the head
	another breath... and just allow your hands to flop down... that's it.	I	drop the hands
	One more breath... and just allow your feet to go to rest...that's good...	I	drop the feet
	And now on the next breath out... just imagine if your chest and spine have turned to jelly... and your whole body like butter left out on a sunny day...		Dissociation
	and that you are so... relaxed... that's excellent... you are doing really well...	D	reassurance
	Vanish the numbers		

	I wonder if you can imagine a tall building... a skyscraper somewhere... at night... and it has ten floors... and each floor is lit up...		
	and with each breath out... you count aloud from ten down to one ... and with each breath out... one floor of that building goes dark... from the top down... and as you breathe out... as each floor goes dark... those numbers begin to disappear until you just can't find the next number...	>	Visualization
	and each breath out takes you down and down... deeper and deeper... darker and darker... that's good...	D	numbers disappear
	and each breath out can make you so relaxed... so comfortable... that's excellent	D	eyelids fluttering
	Test for depth of trance		
	and that fluttering of your eyelids		pacing
	is showing you	>	
	that you are going into trance	D	leading
	and everything is the way it should be...	I	reassurance
	And part of your mind is probably wondering if you are going into trance...		mind reading
	while another part of mind has already gone into the level of trance that is exactly right for you.	>	client can't fail
	I would like you now to pay attention to the little muscles that control your eyelids... those tiny muscles can become so relaxed that you just won't be able to open your eyes... you just can't open those eyes... and when you are sure that those muscles are so relaxed that you just cannot open your eyes... it is as if they are glued together... totally stuck shut... you can try to open them but you will find that they just won't	D	Eye catalepsy test for trance

	work... they just don't open.		
	[*movement of eyebrows*]		
	That's right. And that is showing you that part of your mind can be awake and alert while another part of your mind goes deeply, deeply into trance.	D	trance confirmed
	Personal Power section		
Capability	That's good... and that shows you the power of your mind.	D	
Rule	Maybe you tell yourself you can't be bothered opening them... maybe you just don't want to... maybe you can't... doesn't matter... there are many ways of getting to the result that you want.	>	non sequitur presupposition
Capability	That just shows you the power of your mind. And you can use that power... you can use that power to change things... to imagine things... and allow your mind to roam free and think of things you haven't thought of for a long time... and that means that you can do whatever you want to do...	>	Unspecified outcome
Identity	that shows you that you have a strong mind... and I think you might have known that yourself...	>	confirmation
Capability	and that means you can control parts of your body that you are not even aware of... and you can control parts of your mind you are not aware of...	>	Suggest hidden powers
Capability	And you have control... of anything you want to do... and if you truly want to lose weight then you can give yourself that permission now... decide that the time is now... from this moment on, you are going to enjoy that feeling... of control... you already know what to do...	>	
Identity	and because you have control... you can	>	

	choose to change... Do you want to change [client name]? Do you want to be different from now on?		
	[await response]		Get pledge
	Yes		
	Mirror metaphor section		
	Now just allow your mind to clear...		Dissociation
	I wonder if you can imagine a room... with two mirrors... side by side... and you step in front of one mirror... an old mirror...		
	and in that old mirror you can see yourself as you are now... really look at yourself honestly... and ask yourself, is that honestly how you planned it? How you want to go through life? How you want others to think of you?		
	Or do you want something better?	I	Expectation
	Do you deserve something better?	I	
	and looking in the background...behind you in that mirror... stretching back behind ... you can see a lot of old stuff... all the old stuff that is keeping you like this...		
	and there is the other mirror... a new mirror... and you can step away from that first mirror, the old mirror, and look into this new mirror... and in this new mirror you see yourself... a few weeks or months from now...		Visualization
	and you see someone who is slim, strong, toned, fit... exactly the way you want to be... and you can see yourself in that mirror... your own body... fit and slim... and notice how you are dressed... and the expression on your face...		future rehearsal
	and I wonder what you would call that... satisfaction? confidence? justification? or		

	maybe you know it as something else...		
	What do you call that expression, [client name]? [await response - use the response to motivate by direct suggestion later]		anchoring to an emotion
	[response]		
Capability	and in that look there is [response], and there is knowledge... knowledge that you did this... you can do this... really see yourself in that mirror... look at every part of that new you...	D	
	and you want that body... you want that shape... and to get that shape... to keep that shape... you step briefly to one side... and turn that other mirror, that old mirror, turn it to the wall... so that it no longer reflects... and that old you is no longer there...	D	Metaphoric 'turning away' from old ways
	and can you turn that mirror? [await response]		Confirm-ation
	And the only mirror that works now is the one that shows you the way you want to be	I	ambiguity
Capability	... and you can be that, can't you? You know how to do that, don't you?		tag
	And you can look into the background of that mirror, you can see that things are different now... you can see that a lot of that old stuff has gone now... turning away that other mirror has wiped out so much, old stuff that you don't need anymore. And just think about that now... think about what was in the background of that old mirror ... and just imagine now, that old stuff in the background... shrinking, getting darker, and further away... fading into darkness... and maybe you can imagine yourself walking away from that... towards the bright new mirror...		
	and the old stuff can keep disappearing the		Embedded

	way things do when you look into the rear view mirror of a car... things behind you get smaller and then vanish... Because when you are looking forward, they are not important any more...		metaphor - implied journey
	Because you can turn your back on the past... so you just don't see it any more... turning that old mirror round means that you don't have to take anything with you... and you might be surprised at what or who is missing when you look into that new mirror...	D	
	as you step into that image of the new you... and imagine that you can step into that new mirror... right through that mirror and out the other side...		Action metaphor
	and what you can see now... is the future... and you are in a bright place... and you can see things changing... become exactly the way you want them to be... and you can look backward from that place... looking back into the room... into that dark room... and there may be people in the background... there may be places... they may be familiar... or you may never have noticed them before... but they will seem far away... you can look at them now, see them for what they really are...		
	so take some time now to put things into perspective... decide what you want to have happen to them... you might see some of them leaving... as you realise that some things can be left behind... left to fade... and shrink... to fade from view		Metaphor Transform-ation
	Direct suggestion section		
Capability	because you are in control now... you decide what is important in your life from	>	ambiguity

	now on... and that will help you until... you become compelled to be that person in the new mirror... and there will be new things in your life now... different things... things that you choose to have there...		
Identity	Because you want to live a long and healthy life, don't you? And you want to look good, and you want other people to see you looking good,	D	
Identity	you want to be the person you can be... the person you should be... and that person is strong and slim and toned and tanned and all these other things you want to be... and you can be that.	D	
Identity	And you are going to be that.	D	
Behavior	And you are going to do that from now on.	D	ambiguity
Capability	And there is nothing in your life will stop you doing that now, is there? You can do anything you want.	D	
Capability	And you are going to do it. You are starting now, can't you?	D	
Capability	That's right. You have that ability. You can lose weight. You can exercise.	D	
Identity	You are going to become the person in that mirror. You are going to have that pride, that look...	D	
Memory	And you can look in that new mirror... and just turn to one side, and turn to the other side and just see what you look like, the way you want to look, just rejoice in that, glory in that, feel how good you can feel... How good does that make you feel? Just think of how wonderful you would feel being that...		Visualization
Identity	And you can keep that shape for years and years and years. you can be exactly like	D	Permanence

	that,		
Identity	and take a moment now... see yourself dressed in shorts and gym gear... and you can see yourself as you would be in other situations... how you would be dressed for work, and see yourself now... how you would be dressed for going for an interview or other important things... you can see how you would be dressed going to meet someone romantic, maybe even getting married... In that mirror you can see yourself in all those situations... exactly the way you want to be.	I	Visualize changes
Identity	Because that is your future... that is what you are getting... that is what life has waiting for you...	D	
Capability	you will know how to achieve that... you will just feel this compulsion ... to get on with it... to do it... and you may not know what it is that drives you towards that...		
Memory	but it will all be automatic... like something takes over... you just wake up in the morning and think 'things are different' ...	D	Anchor morning
Capability	'I don't have to be like I let myself be...'	I	was a choice
Capability	And you will go to bed knowing how to do this...	D	Anchor night
Behavior	and all through your day... you will be looking forward to exercise... to going to the gym... to meeting your friends... you could take up sport... think about it now... you could do things in the park... you could do things in the gym... you could go swimming or cycling or running or... anything you want... and you can see yourself doing those things... you have an endless choice...	D	any exercise
Behavior	And you can become obsessive... about using every opportunity... no matter how	D	Method

	small... you could choose to walk more, to use the stairs, stretch at odd moments...		
Behavior	And when you do those things you feel wonderful... you feel really good...	D	Result
	Just imagine how good you will feel... being strong and fit and athletic... feeling that change	K	Outcome
	and who is most surprised when you change? Who it is you could really impress? Imagine what they might have to say... And you can think about that... and that pride...	I	Reinforce desire
Behavior	And you can allow yourself to enjoy those changes ... and look forward to a new lifestyle.		
Identity	And knowing that from this day forward you are taking a step away from the past and into that new bright future... and see it now, in bright colors... as if the sun always shines ... as if every day is perfect...		
	Double dissociation section		
Identity	and see yourself walking along... in the street, maybe... proud, strong... others looking at you sideways... thinking how does he do it... How good would that make you feel about yourself?	V	
Memory	And maybe walking into the gym and feeling at home with everyone there... the younger guys looking at you ... taking notice of you... with approval	V	
Identity	See yourself losing weight... bulking out... muscle... strength... speed... energy... and you want that [client name] don't you? And you are going to have that [client name], aren't you? That's right.	V	
	And you just focus on that mirror... you just focus on looking at how you want to be...	V	Ideal goal

	that perfect, perfect image of yourself.		
Behavior	And maybe you can imagine a path coming back from that image... to where you are now... and you can see every step in that path... you see how you get there... you can see how you do that... you can see yourself gathering the resources you need... picking up the things you want... making that happen, making that a reality... And you can do that...	V	
Behavior	And I think you know that you have started now... you have made that first tiny change... just imagine that tiny change... like a pebble can start an avalanche...	M	
	and that will go on and multiply and increase and change and change.	D	
	And every day is another step towards that image...	D	reframe
	until the day comes when you can step right into that mirror... and just merge into that body and you and it are the same... you are that same person and you have arrived...		
Identity	and you will be like that for ever... exactly how you want to be. And that's a good thing, isn't it?		
	Engine Metaphor section		
Capability	And now [client name] I want you to store all that away... I want you to take that image... take that knowledge... and somehow fuse it right into the core of who you are. Put it in there... become that change... in a way that makes sense to you... and know that that is there for you... always... It is as if some old thing has been replaced in you...	I	

Identity	It is as if you have gone into the workshop and taken the engine out of the car and replaced it with a new and better engine... and that new engine will power on...	
	and although it looks the same to someone outside, the car owner knows it's different, and the performance is different. And that car owner knows that he can just leave the rest standing at the lights... if he wants to... because inside, things have changed... and he knows he just has to tap that accelerator to see a huge change	Reframe
	Future Rehearsal section	
	And so just allow your mind to clear now... allow your mind to clear and just know that you have that knowledge that you have changed... as you whole attitude towards exercise and food and personal care have changed radically... been replaced with something better... and you will always have that image in your mind... that second mirror...	D
Identity	and as you think about it... that other mirror that you turned to the wall... begins to shrink ... and you can watch it shrinking and getting further away from you... and you can see every last remnant of you stepping away ... rejecting that old image and that old stuff... until there is only one mirror left... your mirror...	D
	and you are looking into that mirror and you are looking through that mirror into the future... and you can see a future for yourself I think ... and it's the future the way you want it to be... and you can peer into that and you can look to the left and to the right... and you can see years ahead...	Metaphor

	and you can see things working out the way you really wanted them to... the way you always wanted them to		
Behavior	And see yourself becoming a success... a success socially... a success financially... a success bodily... a success romantically... And see yourself, now, taking your role in society... and giving things back to society... and see yourself developing emotionally and maybe spiritually... and see yourself becoming a full and complete and total member of a family.. and expanding your networks and relationships... And you stand in the centre of that network... strong... proud... doing what you want to do... being what you want to be ... having what you want to have... surrounded by family and friends and close emotional ties... and making a complete success of your life through three hundred and sixty degrees...		
	And in your mind you can turn around... and just look at every aspect of your life... financial and work and social and family and emotional and relationships... and see yourself... see every aspect of your life now... You are happy and fulfilled. You are a planner... You do the things that you want to do... you control your life... you control your time...		
	Physical Metaphor section		
	And somehow now you are able to focus... decide what you want and what you don't want...	D	Ambiguity
	And you know you are surrounded by this network of friends and family... all the people who are important to you... who	D	Visualization

	support you and love you... and you can love them back...		
Capability	And because they love you and you love them back... you can love yourself... you can respect yourself... and self-respect included respect for your body... includes making yourself healthy, strong...	> D	
	And that motivation, I think you can feel it growing now... I think you can feel it now rumbling and sparking like a distant storm... growing and growing and that power is growing in you... that power, that power to do whatever you want... a massive ability just building up... you can feel that now... rising and rising building and building... and you are so full of energy... you can feel your hands beginning to tingle you can feel your fingers beginning to move... you can feel those hands beginning to lift... and those hands are going up and up and up... you can start moving those hands now you can feel them going up ... you can feel that movement in your hands... that's right they are beginning to move up now ... one and two the left and the right... they are rising... they are rising... rising... that determination... that strength... that ability is going up and up and up... and is growing in you... growing like a gathering storm... that cloud of strength and ability... that vast power is there...	D	Storm Metaphor: Pacing and Leading [said with mounting excitement and urgency]
	And when you know that you have absolutely changed at some point it's like there is a crash of lightening and your hands just drop down... and you just let go all that old stuff...	>	Physical affirmation
	[hands drop]		

	That's right... it's over... Well done...	D
	And you can just let out a great breath... a sigh of relief...	
	Healthy Eating section	
Capability	That's right... you have changed forever... it's gone... totally gone... that's very good... and you know that from this moment on... you will have all the motivation you need... to get exercise... to keep your weight under control... and eat properly... and you'll find time to eat properly... you will find yourself actually worrying about the quality of what you eat... actually thinking about balanced meals and insisting that you have a balanced meal... and you will find that junk food has no interest for you any more... and you will always eat at a table... something that is important to you... that you won't eat in front of a television... that you always eat at a table... and wherever possible you like to eat with another person... and you eat slowly... chewing every mouthful... twenty or thirty times... really becoming aware of what you are eating... becoming aware of the taste and the texture... and how good it is for you...	
Behavior	And you can become aware and alert to fatty foods... you don't like fatty foods... you really don't like them... you find yourself pushing them away... and reaching for green healthy food... proper meals... eaten slowly... and if possible enjoyed with someone else... and you think about what you eat... carefully...	
Identity	and there will be times when you just don't feel like eating... you just can't be bothered... rather than eat something that is bad for	

63

	you, you just skip it... and you won't even notice...	
	and you will just become aware that your clothes are loose on you	
	Direct suggestion: eating healthy	
	and you have this powerful desire to exercise now... and you look forward to the time and the days and the hours when you can exercise... taking part in that... and at lunchtimes and other breaks you find yourself wanting to go for a walk... if you can... maybe just walking up and down the stairs a few times... and you do that instead of snacking and you find yourself really enjoying fruit... looking forward to it ... slowly eating a crunchy apple... and feeling the texture in your mouth... that crumbly sweet taste... that taste of health... and you can feel it doing you good... and you can enjoy slowly taking an orange... feeling the dimpled skin under your fingers... smelling that citrusy aroma... the oil squirts as you cut into it... and the juice rolls down the side... and maybe you cut it carefully into eight sections... and you can imagine lifting that to your mouth... biting into the yellow flesh... smelling the orange juice... feeling it running into your mouth... some on your chin... and you feel like throwing your head back and laughing it tastes so good...	
	And you know you love healthy food... you have always got time to eat that... and you see yourself rejecting other stuff... it's not important...	
	Because you want to live a long and healthy life, don't you? And that's the way to a long and healthy life, isn't it? That's right... And	

	you have already taken that decision. You have that strength... that power... you've got all the motivation you need... I think you can feel that tingling in your fingers now.	
	It's that feeling that you can do anything you want. And that combination of good eating, good exercise... good friends... is going to give you everything you want. in the future... and you know that don't you? That's right.	
Identity	And you know that things have changed. And you have changed.	
Capability	And you can see yourself somehow... reaching out into the future and taking what you want... like picking an apple off a tree... being what you want... and knowing that that belongs to you... You deserve it... You can do that... You are doing it now... it's easy...	
Identity	And that's who you are...	
	Step into the mirror...	echo of metaphor
	Reorientation	
	So in a moment I am going to count from five to one... and when I get to one... you will be back in the present feeling refreshed and fully awake and ready for the rest of your day.	
Capability	And knowing that something fundamental has changed...	
Identity	And knowing that deep down inside there is that new thing... that new vision... that new you...	echo of metaphor
Capability	And you have that fierce determination like a storm taking you there... now.	echo of metaphor
	FIVE	

	FOUR beginning to get feeling back into your arms and legs...		
	THREE... taking a deep breath... head moving... arms moving		
	and TWO getting ready for a yawn and a stretch feeling really good... eyelids flickering...		
	And ONE EYES OPEN back to the present fully alert ready for the rest of your day.		

Change the past

This script is designed to get rid of things that happened in the past and lets you change how you experience the past. Hypnotherapy is a powerful way of releasing old hurts and emotional abuse so you can move on in life. This metaphor therapy allows the person to uncover old things that they might not even be aware were a problem, and to safely watch as they happen and then to change the past. It uses a metaphor of a mirror in a room that reflects differently and that can change the past.

You can't change the past, but you can change how you remember the past, and how you let it affect you. This hypnotic metaphor sets up the old event, then switches attention to a different view, then the person is given the power to change the past, and the new perspective takes over.

Target	Kinesthetic Induction Section		
	Now take a deep breath... hold it... and let it out...		
	And another breath... and as you breathe out... really relax...		
	and one more and let your whole body relax... that's right...		
	now become aware of the weight of your body... your arms and legs can go heavy... imagine how they would feel if they were so heavy you just can't lift them...		Relax the body
	and allow yourself to settle down deeper now...		
	Dissociation Induction Section		
Memory	I wonder if you can remember a child's picture book? The sort of book that has picture and stories and different scenes and different places...	V	Dissociation
	imagine opening that book ... and there is a page with a scene outdoors... somewhere in		

	the countryside... on a hot sunny day...		
	and someone lying in the shade there enjoying the warmth and relaxation...		
	and imagine now... as you relax... even more... a different page... and there's a warm fire burning in a comfortable room... and a big armchair to settle down in...	V	
	and imagine now resting in that armchair... feeling relaxed and comfortable ... in that calm peaceful place... and allow your mind to drift off...	K	
	to a page with a tree... a big tree somewhere ... and that tree has roots going down... imagine those roots going deep down into the earth... going back a long way... imagine those roots spreading out... ever wider... ever deeper... and allow your mind to go deeper... letting go... thinking of those deep roots...		
	Mirror transformation metaphor	e	
	and you find yourself walking along a road in the countryside... and there is a wall beside the road... and you follow along the wall, a high wall... surrounding something important...		something hidden
	and you come to a gate... a big wide gate... and the gate begins to open... and there is path a driveway beyond the gate... and the driveway leads you on...		a way in
	and the path goes through trees and bushes and then round a corner...		indirection
	and you come to a building... a big important looking building... and there are smaller buildings nearby... a pond... bits of machinery lying around... a barn...		lots of resources
	and you go up to the main building... and you reach out and touch the wall... and you		guiding the unconscious

	feel the surface ... and you trail your hand along the wall... just letting it take you wherever it leads...		
	and as you touch that wall... your mind is drifting back in time... to a long time ago... to time when something happened to you... that has never been cleared... something that should not have happened to you... the way it did... something important that it is time to change...		leads to the problem
	and you come to a window... and you look in the window... and you are looking into a room...	M	metaphor room = life
	and in that room there is something going on... something important... and it is a scene from your own life... something that has affected your life... and you can watch as this scene appears in that room... you are a spectator... just looking... watching... as if it was happening to someone else...		Dissociation
	you can see everything that is going on... the people... the place... you are aware of how you feel... how it affected you... something that hurt you is going on in that room... you can see it, experience it... as if it was happening right now...		revivification
	But on the back wall there is a mirror... and that mirror is reflecting what is going on in the room... but you can see the room and you can see the mirror and the room in the mirror...		Double dissociation
	but as you watch... as you are looking through the window... the mirror starts to get bigger... and in it things get clearer... and the things in the mirror somehow are not exactly the same as the things in the room...		magic resource for change
Capability	And you realize that because you are		Power to

	looking in the room this time... things are getting changed... and you realize that you can see the room and you can see the mirror... and you can influence what the mirror shows... you can make things in the mirror turn out differently... turn out the way you want them to... the way they should have turned out...	change the past
	so you can see the room... the way things were... and you can see the mirror... the way things can be... and you have the ability to change what happens in the mirror... and you can take a few moments now to choose, to decide how it should have ended... what would be the best outcome for you... what you deserved to have happen... and change it in the mirror now... until you are completely satisfied with how things should be...	double perspective on the event
	and as you make those changes... the mirror gets bigger and brighter... and the events in the room begin to lose focus... to start to melt and dim... and as the mirror gets brighter... the room dims and getter darker... and things start to melt away... and soon there the events in the room can hardly be seen, and vanish... and the light from the mirror replaces everything in that room...	replace the old version with the new
	And when you are ready ... you can lower the curtain on that scene... and move away from the window... knowing that things have changed forever... changed to the way they should have been...	let it face away
	and a part of you knows that something deep inside has changed.	
	[use direct suggestion for the specific problem here]	

	Reorientation	
Capability	And when you are ready... when you have done everything you need to do... made all the transformations you want to see... felt the difference of being different...	I
Identity	And knowing that something really has changed...	
	that deep down inside there is something... opening... loosening...	
	Then you can begin the process of coming back to the present... but in the meantime... take whatever time you need...	
	and then count to yourself from five up to one... and when you get to one, you will be back in the present, fully alert, and ready for the rest of your day...	
	So just take as long as you need now...and come back to the present when you know that the process of change is starting and will continue...	

Relaxation for Weight Loss

This script uses the idea of relaxing to induce trance and at each stage of the progressive muscle relaxation adds a set of suggestions about how to lose weight and get healthy.
Then the script has a section of direct suggestions followed by an extended metaphor about a healing light loosening the excess weight and preparing the body to lose it.

Target	Set up		Comments
	Please do not listen to this recording while you are driving or doing anything that requires your full attention.		Safety
	If you have any medical problems please consult your doctor before using this recording.		Safety
	Make sure you are in some place where you can relax completely in safety, and where you won't be disturbed for half an hour or so.		
	Induction section		
	This session will teach you how to relax... everyone accepts that relaxing is good... and losing weight is good... so now you can learn to relax and use that relaxation for weight control... now that's really good... isn't it?	I	Suggestion
Capability	Your body has the natural ability to relax completely... and effortlessly... so you can just let go...	=	
	so, settle into a very comfortable position, you can be sitting or lying down, it really doesn't matter... as long as you are getting comfortable.	I	
Capability	and as you make yourself comfortable you can give a signal to your body and mind to let them know that you are preparing to	I	Pre-supposition

	relax now		
Capability	You can relax without any effort at all.	D	
Capability	Your mind has the capacity to relax completely... which means your mind can empty now...	=	
	and from now on, as you are listening to these words, those words will soothe and comfort, and relax... Every sound you hear will make you more comfortable... more at ease...	I	Deepener
	When I say relax, that means let go of everything... relax your body... relax your mind... completely...	D	
	And as you relax... all the stress and the tensions of the day are leaving your body... falling away... leaving you feeling good... relaxed... peaceful... calm...	K	
	Progressive muscle relaxation		
	So just let it all go now... and allow your eyes to close... imagine those eyelids getting heavier and heavier... image those eyelids coming down... like a leaf falling from a tree... and now that your eyes are gently closed... those eyes can relax even more.	M	Eye closure
	And now your eyes are relaxed, feel that relaxation flowing up to your forehead. Relax all the muscles in your forehead. Imagine a gentle hand stroking across your skin... easing and soothing...	K	Relax the head
	Now let that relaxation flow and spread from your forehead to the top of your head. Feel your scalp relax... completely loose and relaxed.	K	
	Now feel the muscles of your face becoming loose, relaxed. Relax your facial muscles, relax your jaw... all the muscles around your	K	

	lips and chin.		
	That's right. And image what a smile would feel like with a perfectly relaxed face... Your smile is going to be wonderful... soft and relaxed now.	K	Reassurance
	Feel this relaxation spreading in your mind. All you have to do is let it go, let it happen.	K	
	And every word, every sound is making you even more relaxed.	D	deepener
	You are just letting things go and drifting into a very deep, very relaxed, very comfortable state of mind. You are doing it just right.	K	reassurance
	And at this time, if any thoughts come into your mind, you can simply ignore them.		Relax the mind
	Just letting it go now.		
	Now focus on relaxing all the parts of your body. Relax all the muscles of your neck, let all the tightness and tension around your neck area be completely gone...	K	Neck
	feel this relaxation moving down your body like wave... Relax all the muscles, big and small, around your shoulders.	K	Shoulders
	Let any weight, any feeling of duties, responsibilities... be gone completely from your shoulders and the neck area. You are feeling a wonderful sense of freedom, lightness around your shoulders. Relax.	K	
	Now feel this relaxation flowing down to your upper arms. Let all the muscles in your upper arms go completely relaxed. Let this relaxation flow down to your elbows ... to your lower arms...		Arms
	flowing down to your hands and fingers. Your fingers are completely relaxed, totally relaxed, and you don't even feel them, that is		Hands

	wonderful.		
	And the more you relax the more your body becomes naturally feels heavy and peaceful and calm.		Deepener
Capability	And right now you are feeling peace, calmness, enjoying the quiet energy all around you, just by letting things go.	D	
Capability	All the organs of your body can renew themselves, get new energy, new power when you simply let things go... doing absolutely nothing ... simply relaxing...	V	
	all the stress, all the tensions of the day are leaving your body and mind.	D	
	Now, let your chest relax. Release any tension, any pressure from that area. Far away, feel the gentle beat of your pulse... like the wings of a tiny bird, taking you deeper and deeper...	K	Chest
Memory	And as you let go... let go of emotions from the past, negative emotions, any kind of past negative experience, you can simply let them go. Let any hatred, anger or restlessness let go... relax your body and mind completely.	>	Release old feelings
Memory	You are doing just great, and remember that the past is past, so allow any negative emotions to flow out of your body ... release that negative energy from your mind. Feel the exchange of peace and divine blessings.	K	Release old memories
	And within that calmness... forgive others and forgive yourself. Forgiveness can feel wonderful. When you forgive rightly you feel the peace and energy gathering within.	D	Forgiveness
	Right now, focus on feeling wonderful... think about any pain you are holding... and forgive those who caused it ... feel the energy and blessings of forgiveness... because forgiveness is about you... about	D	Releasing pain

	making things right... about making you right... right now... letting go of that pain...		
	And now let the relaxation flow down to your tummy. Picture all the internal organs relaxing now. With every breath you are you are feeling lighter... a new energy a new peace of mind.		Abdomen
Belief	And now allow that natural love for yourself to emerge... because you deserve love and the moment you experience that love... your body and mind become one... in perfect harmony.	>	Giving Love
	And now this relaxation is flowing down to your hips and thighs. Relax and feel wonderful. Let all the stress, all the tensions flow out... bringing out your natural health and strength.		Hips
	Now, very gently let this relaxation flow all the way down to your lower legs And the body from top of your head to the tips of toes you are completely relaxed... feeling good.		Legs
Behavior	You know that you have decided to lose that extra weight and extra inches.	D	
Capability	Your subconscious mind, as you already know, has all the power and wisdom you need to achieve this simple goal.	D	
Behavior	And from now on, you find yourself every morning in the mood for a walk or to go jogging.	D	Exercise
	You can see yourself outdoors in good weather or working out indoors.	V	
Belief	You find that you now love to do a physical workout every day. You tell yourself 'I love my exercises'.	D	Exercise
Belief	Exercise makes you relaxed, energetic and	D	

	happy.		
Belief	And you feel wonderful doing this new habit every day.	D	
Capability	And this new activity is making you slimmer and healthier. You are becoming the person you want to be, exactly the size and weight you want to be.	D	Exercise
Behavior	Daily walks are becoming a habit. Exercise is fun. Getting active puts a smile on your face.	D	Exercise
Belief	Exercise makes you want to eat better.	D	Eating
Behavior	See yourself eating breakfast... very slowly, you like to eat slowly now.	V	Eating
Belief	and that makes your digestion and metabolism healthy.	>	
Behavior	And eating your midday meal, you eat slowly and you eat less. You find yourself thinking about what you are eating... and that makes your midday meal satisfying to your body and mind.	>	Eating
Behavior	And the evening meal... You are eating it slowly... with love in every bite... love for who you are... love for your body... for what you are becoming... loving your new life...	D	Eating
Behavior	From now on you eat only three times a day: at breakfast, lunch and evening.	D	Eating
Behavior	That is the only time you eat. Eating at other times makes you feel bad.	D	Eating
Belief	Good eating makes you want to lose that extra weight and extra inches.	D	Eating
Behavior	Eating only three times a day is easy for you now.	D	Eating
Belief	Your subconscious mind fully understands your desire to be the right weight and right shape and is working on that for you now.	D	

	Imagine yourself in your new life.	V	Visualization
Behavior	eating slowing, at the right time, and eating with care and attention.	D	Eating
Behavior	You drink water or juice with meals. Drinking lots of water has become part of your new life.	D	Diet
Behavior	You love to be physically active, exercising in many ways. Knowing this is leading to what you want.	D	Exercise
Behavior	Every bit of exercise is taking off those inches… making you healthier…		
	See yourself achieving your goal… approaching your ideal weight… the natural and easy way…	V	Progress
Belief	You respect yourself, you respect your body, you respect your mind… and that is leading you to do the right things…	>	
Belief	And as you lose weight… everything can get easier… things are going right for you… at home… at work…	>	
Belief	Your subconscious mind is listening right now. Your subconscious mind has all the power you will ever need. And it is working for you right now. You don't need willpower, you don't need to do anything. Trust your own mind to look after you. Trusting your own mind means you can get healthy quickly and easily.	D	Resource
Memory	You know, when you look back, it doesn't matter what you did in the past, what mistakes you made, your future is about eating well… being well… living well.	D	Reassurance
	You are now losing weight every day,	D	Affirmation
	You are becoming what you always wanted to be.	D	Affirmation

	You are learning to relax and be open to love wherever it comes from.	D	Affirmation
	Every day your confidence increases.	D	Affirmation
	You have more energy, more ideas, more fun each day.	D	Affirmation
	You are breathing easy, learning to relax with every breath.	D	Affirmation
	Your body is changing, your skin is glowing, you are getting healthier in every way.	D	Affirmation
	Now take a deep breath and relax... that's right		
	And as you breathe out... imagine what it would feel like to be covered in a fine colored light... feel the warmth of its touch... feel yourself being bathed in this healing light.	K	Resource
	Now imagine this light all around you... feel it cleansing and energising the cells of your body... feel it gently penetrating your skin... your flesh... your muscles... notice how it moves and spreads... and feel how it is loosening the excess weight from all over your body.	K	Metaphor
Capability	Feel how the touch of this light transforms your flesh... moving, changing, releasing... and realize that this light is the power of your mind... your mind has the power to change your body... body and mind are one.	K	Resource
	And knowing that can leave you feeling a new energy and new peace and calmness in your body and mind.	I	Resource
Belief	And you deserve this wonderful feeling, you deserve to be healthy... to be fit and slim...	D	
Behavior	Every day is a new day... a day to celebrate... becoming a celebrity... Everything you do is making you more attractive... Your life		Celebrate success

	becoming filled with love and pleasure... and that is giving you a new energy, a new confidence... every day you eat properly, every day you find time to exercise... is a success... so your days are filled with success.	
	And allow that to fade... leaving an afterglow of deep, deep relaxation in every part of you...	
	Reorientation	
	And now you can begin to think about coming back to the present... bringing with that calm... that knowledge that you have changed... that feeling of letting go everything that was holding you back.	Reorientation
	So now gently let yourself return to full alertness... feel yourself stirring... getting ready to stretch... eyelids fluttering...	
	Back the present... eyes open... WIDE AWAKE NOW!	

Better Eating Habits

This script puts the client into trance and then uses a series of indirect and direct suggestion for getting and keeping better eating habits. Each of the better eating strategies is based on scientifically proven evidence. Anyone who follows the advice must lose weight.

	Now relax and get ready to enjoy this easy way to lose weight...		Supposition
	Settle down comfortably now... all you have to do is listen... everything will happen for you... easily, effortlessly... you don't have to do anything except relax...		reassurance
	I am going to help you... to relax deeply...		Anticipation
	to have access to the most powerful part of your mind...		Resource
	To your subconscious mind... the part of your mind that regulates your body ...	I	Anticipation
	Breathing Induction		
	Now let's begin... become aware of your breathing... focus your attention on your breathing... just slowly breathing in and out...		Focus on breathing
	Just allow your breathing to slow down... natural and relaxing...		breathing
	Slowly breathing in and out...		
	and as you release that breath... allow your eyes to close		eye closure
	And with each breath... feel yourself becoming more and more relaxed... more deeply relaxed... and every word you hear... is making you more relaxed still...		breathing
	And as you breathe in... imagine a feeling of confidence, well-being and peacefulness within you...		breathing
	Imagine what it would be like if your body...	V	Dissociation

81

	was floating on a fluffy cloud...		
	And you are floating effortlessly... calmly drifting away now...	K	Leave body
	And as you feel yourself... going deeper and deeper... allow any thoughts to gently let go...	K	Empty the mind
	You're feeling the stillness and absolute peace and tranquility... like never before ... and relaxing deeper and deeper...		Deepener
	Progressive Muscle Induction		
	You are feeling blissfully relaxed... without a care in the world...		
	and filled with healing energy... and the whole of your body... is being flooded with wonderful healing energy...		Energy
	Feel a healing... loving energy... flowing through your body... from your head... all the way down to your toes...		Energy
	and imagine that energy flowing ... down through your body...		Energy
	and mentally follow that healing energy as it washes away all those things that were keeping you back...		Energy
	as if the weight of it was draining away all your cares... all your worries... flowing down past your chest... down towards your thighs... down your legs... draining right out of your body...		cleansing
	Your body, mind and spirit... are in perfect harmony now...		harmony
	Your whole body is relaxing now... deeply relaxed... and in tune with the abundance of health and wealth from the Universe... a universe filled with love and forgiveness...		harmony
Capability	And when you are in this state... your mind can reveal its hidden power...		

	Release Tension		
	as you become more deeply relaxed... with each gentle breath... deep within your body... your whole being... is being filled with confidence, health, happiness...		
	and become aware of any tensions in your body... And as you breathe out... feel all that tension... all that stress... leaving your body... just breathe it out... let that stress drift away...	K	Release tension
	And as you leave the stresses of the day behind... you are present in the Now... and Now is all that matters... right Now... as you relax deeper and deeper...		Deepener
	It's a wonderful feeling... being in the Present... in an unbounded state of absolute bliss and peace...	l	
	You are now seeing yourself and the world in a more harmonious, liberated, happy way... and that means you are changing...	>	Reframing
	Feel all that love and forgiveness flowing to wherever there are negative emotions... for yourself... your family... anyone...		Forgiving
	Forgiveness feels so wonderful... By forgiving... you let go of so much... stress and tension...		Forgiveness
	any guilt any negative emotions... simply let them go... and they will be gone forever		Forgiveness
	Future Pacing		
	Now when you wake up in the morning... you'll feel more energy and confidence... more enthusiasm for your day ahead...		wakening
Behavior	First thing in the morning...you'll have a high fiber drink... and then drink a large glass of water... You'll start drinking more and more water during the day...		fiber

83

Behavior	Your meals will include more low fat protein foods... like chicken, fish and lean meat... or vegetarian protein... like Tofu... beans and lentils... you eat high fiber foods... at every meal... It's good to have some form of protein with every meal... and plenty of raw fruits and vegetables...		Fiber
Behavior	Your midday meal... and evening meals... also include healthy protein... maybe a salad... and brown rice... or wholemeal bread... and you are naturally eating more whole grain foods...		Better eating
Behavior	and as you eat better... you find you are losing interest in junk food like white flour, white rice... and sugar... and convenience foods... junk foods do not interest you any more... they are an echo of the past...		Better eating
Behavior	And you will avoid soda and other sweet drinks because you know that corn syrup stops your body knowing when you are full.		Better eating
	Eat the right things and enjoy your food ...The more you move to natural unprocessed foods... the more you lose weight effortlessly... that's right, effortlessly	>	natural foods
	Supplement Advert [insert supplement name]		
	You are now introducing -[Unrefined Virgin Coconut oil]... into your daily food...		supplement
	[Virgin Coconut Oil] is the Secret ingredient... to Effortless Weight loss... Just consume [portion size] every day... and use it as your preferred ingredient in cooking... You'll be amazed how good your food tastes...		supplement
	[Virgin Coconut Oil]... speeds up your metabolism... and improves Thyroid function... and helps to burn fat... and gives		supplement

	you more energy... What a wonderful natural product...		
	Thousands of people like yourself have discovered the Weight Loss miracle of [Virgin Coconut Oil]... by adding [portion size] to their healthy food choices...		supplement
	Visualization Section		
	Diet is a word of the past... You are now so much more aware in control and in tune with your body that you automatically make the right healthy food choices... and you will enjoy your healthy food so much more... So much more satisfying taste and texture.		natural foods
Behavior	and you'll start to do some exercise... you'll just feel like doing it... maybe walking or slow running... any exercise you enjoy... You can exercise outside... or indoors... maybe you would like Yoga classes... or join a Gym... think about a Personal Trainer... there are many ways to help you with your journey...		exercise
	Imagine how good you will feel after exercise... you can look forward to a health drink... or a Protein shake...	V	future pacing
	and you will feel full of energy for the day...	V	food
	With you losing weight now and looking and feeling terrific...	V	
V	You will feel wonderful when your friends comment on how much slimmer and healthier you are looking...	V	
	Better Eating Habits		
	And you follow these simple rules to lose weight effortlessly... repeat these in your mind to lose weight effortlessly...		
	Each time I sit down to eat... call up this feeling of total relaxation before I begin...		relax before eating

85

	I now eat slowly and mindfully... I make myself conscious of the food I am eating ... its taste... its texture... its feel... knowing that it is doing me good...	mindfulness
	I focus on the first three bites, really paying attention to what I am experiencing, so my mind believes I am full.	Focus
	I chew my food slowly... and thoughtfully... at least 12 times per mouthful... and really notice the taste of what I am eating...	chewing
	I put my knife and fork down between mouthfuls... and only when I have swallowed and waited for my mouth to clear do I have the next mouthful...	pacing
	I always use the smallest utensils I can... smaller spoons mean smaller mouthfuls...	Smaller utensils
	And for one meal a day, I hold my utensils in the opposite hands to remind me to slow down and enjoy my food.	Swap hands
	I sip water between bites so I never confuse dehydration with hunger.	water
	I try to eat with others... conversation slows down my eating...	Company
	I add spices and hot sauces to wake up my brain and focus on the taste.	Spices
	I drink water or tea with my meals because it makes me feel fuller faster.	Drinks
	I wait twenty minutes after eating my portion before adding anything else to the meal...	Delay
	Indirect Suggestion Section	
	You'll be surprised how effortlessly your weight will melt away... and you'll feel so much healthier, trim, energetic and alive...	I
	Every day... feeling healthier, lighter and happier...	I Affirmations

	And you have more energy to exercise every day... and you are now starting to love exercise...	I	Affirmations
	And you love the feeling of being fit and healthy... and how your clothes are starting to feel loose on you...	I	Affirmations
	Direct Suggestion Section		
	You are becoming a more vigorous, vital, energetic... slimmer new you...	D	
	You are feeling d more and more relaxed in your everyday life...	D	
	Your self-confidence, how you feel about yourself is increasing day by day... and you are feeling happier in many ways...	D	
Capability	Your entire life can change magically... by the choices you make...	D	
Identity	You are unique and wonderful... there is nobody else in this world like you...	D	
	You become what you think about... Start dreaming now... starting think of what could be... and make it a reality...	D	
	Change your thoughts and you can change your life forever...	D	Affirmation
Rule	If you can think it... you can achieve it...Yes you can...	D	Affirmation
	you are now on the way to a new slimmer, more successful you...	D	
	you will be successful in achieving everything you want... and I think part of you knows that too...		
	Reorientation		
	Now it's time... to gently stretch... very gently stretch and open your eyes... and feel love and kindness... for yourself		
	You'll feel a more relaxed, peaceful and calm		

	person... This blissful relaxed feeling will continue with you throughout the day... You'll feel so much lighter and brighter...	
	You can also now go to sleep... if you so desire...	
	And when you wake up... in the morning... You will feel refreshed... and full of energy... ready for a new day and fresh beginnings...	

Stop eating chocolate

Many clients who are overweight say that that they are addicted to some food, like ice cream or cakes or chocolate. They say they could stop eating that food if hypnotherapy could just make it taste horrible.

This Stop Eating Aversion script uses hypnosis suggestions to make the chocolate taste bad. It creates aversion suggestions for all the sensations of sight, smell, taste and texture so the smell is nauseating, the sight is repulsive, the feel is horrible and the very idea of eating chocolate makes you want to vomit. Every aspect of eating chocolate makes you want to get away from it and stay away. The Stop eating chocolate Aversion script makes even the idea of putting chocolate in your mouth revolting.

The script can be easily adapted to any particular food, not just chocolate.

	Breathing Induction		
	Now just close your eyes and relax.		
	Focus on your breathing... and as you breathe out... count each breath, quietly to yourself... counting from one to ten... and after each breath, feel yourself relaxing more and more...		
	[Pause for four breaths]		
	And as you are relaxing there, I wonder if you can imagine being on a hillside somewhere... on a nice day... just imagine you are somewhere in the country on a nice day...	V	
	and as you walk along you come to this sort of valley ... amongst the hills... And down below it all looks cool and inviting...		
	and there is a path going down... and you begin to go down that path... and as you go	M	

	down that path you feel things begin to change... to get cool and dark and secluded... and you feel comfortable... relaxed... as you go down		
	and you come to some water and the water is trickling down rocks like a little waterfall all mossy and soft and gentle... and at the bottom there is a pool...		
	And by the side of the waterfall there are steps going down to that pool... and you begin to go down those steps...		
	Countdown induction		
	and there are ten steps down... and as you go down... each step makes you more relaxed... more at ease... and going down those steps now... Ten... nine... more and more relaxed... and eight ... and seven... relaxing deeper and deeper... and six... and five... and four... and three... deeper and deeper... and two... and one...		Pace with breathing
	and then you are at the pool... and at the pool you begin to think about drifting deeper still ... and you begin to dream about the pool and what is deep down inside...	V	
	Taste aversion Therapy Section		
Memory	and you see yourself reflected in that pool... and you see yourself there... going through your day... thinking about chocolate in the morning... and then eating one or two pieces during the day ... and then going home... and tearing open a chocolate bar... and you see yourself going through all the normal things to do with your day ... and eating chocolate... thinking about chocolate...	V	
	And then everything goes dark... and it's another day... but this day is different...		Transition

	on this other day you decide to touch the water... and ripples go across the pool... and that changes all the images...	M	
	and on this day you see yourself reaching for the chocolate... you see yourself opening the packet... you see yourself picking up the chocolate... bringing it up to your mouth... ... no not quite putting it in your mouth... you see yourself as you pick up that chocolate... but there is something different about it... it looks the same and feels the same but it is not the same...		Strangeness
	and as you bring it close to your mouth... you smell the chocolate... and it touches your tongue... and you feel the chocolate change in your mouth... and you suddenly feel as if some kind of monster has emerged from that chocolate... and it is as if you realize for the first time that it is trying to take hold of you... and it is filling your mouth and throat and as you try to get rid of it... you are feeling it in there like hooks... like a cat clawing at you... like being cut by a knife... and you spit the chocolate out...	K	Kinesthetic aversion
	and you have the most horrible taste in your mouth... that chocolate tastes greasy and sticky... as if you have been eating road kill... as you picked up some slimy maggoty thing and put it in your mouth... you just want to spit it out.. absolutely revolting		
	you just want to run away and brush your teeth... and you get to the bathroom you brush your teeth... and you look in the mirror... and you smile... and you know that you have been saved from that horrible cigarette...		
	it's like all that stuff going down the drain is	M	

	that monster being washed away ...swirling around... and disappearing into some dark place where it dies and loses its power...	
Behavior	And you take a glass of water and you rinse your mouth out... and you feel clean... and fresh...	Action
	and the taste of chocolate disgusts you now	D
	Proximity aversion Therapy Section	
	And you are looking in that pool again on that day... and once again you are going through your day... and you see yourself in a supermarket... or in shop... or a vending machine... and then you become aware of a presence... lurking	
	Like some evil force trying to get you to eat again... and once again it is as if you don't notice and you reach out and you take the chocolate but as soon as you touch it... as soon as you take it out of the wrapper... you realize there is something wrong.. this is not right...	
	and as you think about putting it near your mouth... you suddenly feel your lips... as if they are burning...	
	as if you have some burning chemical on your lips... those lips start to feel hot... throbbing and breaking open... you feel as though those lips are breaking open in huge sores as the chocolate gets closer..	
	and once again... you smell the chocolate and the touch of it is revolting... and you throw it back in the face of that thing that is trying to make you smoke again...	
	and you splash your face with water... and those lips cool down... and heal and you look in the mirror.. and once again you	

	smile... that smile of triumph... of success...	
	and memory of the pain in your lips as you brought the chocolate near... remains with you ... and you know you will never forget that feeling...	
	you don't want to be anywhere near chocolate now...	D
	Touch aversion Therapy Section	
	And once again you look in that pool... and once again you see yourself going through your day... and once again that feeling comes over you... I have to have chocolate... and you see yourself going outside...	V
Behavior	and you reach to get the packet... and even as you think about the packet... as you open it you begin to feel nauseous... you begin to feel a wave of bad feeling coming out of that packet... you see the chocolate there... and it just makes you want to vomit... just the touch of the chocolate is revolting...	
	and imaging holding that chocolate it seems to be some slimy living thing... like a snake coiling round your arm trying to get up to your mouth and you just throw it away...	M
	you throw it on the ground and you stamp it out... you stamp it into pieces and grind it down.. and that makes you feel safe..	>
	and you throw the package away... you throw it away some place where you are free from it... where it will be destroyed...	M
	and you walk away feeling relieved... and that horror you were feeling in your mouth... and you imagine a sink and a toothbrush and brushing your teeth... and so clean... it feels right...	
	and just the thought of it makes you feel ill	

	and you reject it... and walk away...		
	Eating chocolate aversion Therapy Section		
	And you look back in that pool... and you see yourself at night... going home ... going to bed... and you think about the habit you used to have of having chocolate..		
	and just thinking about it now... that idea of putting one in your mouth or having some near you just makes you feel disgusted.. ill...		
	you just want to get away from it... and you know what to do now... any time you have that feeling... you know that you just brush your teeth... it's like magic... the feeling goes away... and you rinse your mouth out with water... spit it out... and you are spitting away all that unhealthy desire...		Spitting out = rejecting chocolate
Memory	You think about all those warnings about sugar and fat... and you know they are right...	V	
	you just know that that is the end of it... that you never want that horrible taste in your mouth again.. that revolting taste... that pain on your lips... that nauseating feeling... that dizziness... that you get from that ... you reject them all...		
Behavior	you reject that totally... chocolate have no place in your life now...	D	
Behavior	even the idea of chocolate makes you feel ill... and you reject them all...		
	and when you see other people eating chocolate... or drinking chocolate... it just turns you off totally...	D	
Behavior	you just want to get away from there... get outside and get some clean air... take a glass of water...	>	
	Social aversion Therapy Section		

	It is getting easier and easier now	D	
	you want nothing to do with chocolate	D	Reframe
Behavior	Your body rejects it... your body rejects everything about chocolate and eating chocolate and chocolate flavors... the sight of chocolate revolts you... Adverts for chocolate anger you...	D	
Behavior	you can be around people eat chocolate... you don't care... they've got problems... let them deal with them... you just let them get on with it... you can succeed	D	
	and any time someone mentions chocolate... chocolate cookies... chocolate cake... chocolate drinks... you get that horrible feeling again...	D	
Behavior	you push the idea away... and you say 'No! no, they make me sick'...' I can't stand the idea of what it is doing to my body'... so you just turn away... and you are safe... and every time you do that... it gets easier...	>	Physical metaphor
	And you can feel safe all through your day... none of this bothers you any more... because you are free...	D	
	Reinforcement of not eating chocolate		
	And looking in that pool again... you see another you reflected there... on another day... you see a day when you wake up with big smile...		
	and you stretch and you get out of bed... and you feel good and you go to the bathroom and you take a glass of water and you swirl it round spit it out you remind yourself of how good it is to be eating properly..		
	that never again will you have to put up with that disgusting stuff	D	
	and you smile in the mirror... and face smiles	V	Desired

	back at you... happy content and sure		state
Capability	and you say to the mirror 'this is easy... I know how to do this... and the strange thing is that when you walk away from that mirror you forget all about chocolate and eating chocolate...	D	Affirmations
Memory	and you see yourself going through your day normally... and all the things you used to do but there are no chocolate there now... and anything that reminds you .. you just don't see it... it is as if you have just wiped it all away...		PHS amnesia
Capability	and you can go through the rest of your day enjoying it all.. you can laugh at that habit...		
Capability	it is like every evening... you now know how to just brush it away... 'get out of my way... I am free'...		
	and as you do, that old feeling... that old need, just withers away... and dies... and you are safe again... happy... another day... healthy and confident...	D	
	Reorientation		
	And imagine ending that day... going to bed... and in that bed sleeping... dreaming... dreaming of someone beside a pool... in a dark valley... and that someone realizes that in fact they are waking up...		
	and it all just seems like a dream... a dream of power and energy... and so begin now to go back up those steps... from one up to ten... and as you do you feel yourself walking away from that habit... leaving it down there and walking up those steps now		
	One, two, three, four, five... and at five you can look back on that habit and see it for what it is... horrible thing... a horrible thing		

	that disgusts you... and walking up towards that sunlight now... is destroying that old thing... it is dying there behind you now...	
	and you are getting ready to come back to the present...six and seven and eight.. almost back into the light... knowing that you have left it all behind...	
	and nine and ten, back into that sunlit hillside stand there and open your arms and take in a great breath of the clean fresh air and now that you are free, see all the world around you as far as you can see... free, clean and clear...	
	and when you are ready... open your eyes and come back to the present... NOW.	

Emotional Release hypnotherapy

This hypnosis script is for people who feel bad and don't really know why they are feeling grumpy or out of sorts or why they are hurting themself and other people. That sort of behavior happens when some event, or something somebody does to you, triggers old feelings of powerlessness, helplessness, injustice, or whatever, and that sets of cluster of familiar destructive behavior. This script is especially useful for hypnotherapy where client has started drinking again, some other habit or behavior they thought they had left behind but comes back and they don't really know why, but they know that something set it off.
The script is an updated version of the Affect Bridge. You get the client to feel the bad feelings and then to visualize those bad feelings as a thing, an object. Then by encouraging them to change the object, they are actually changing the feelings. It is direct way of doing what is usually done with Regression to Cause hypnotherapy.

	Preparation	
	Now before you settle down... I want to think about the things that have been happening in your life that have been causing you distress...	Bind
Memory	become aware of the feelings that you have been having... bring to mind now... how everything seems to be wrong... negative...	
	and consider to what extent it actually what is happening in your own mind that is the problem... that in fact that you are projecting on to the world some inner turmoil... some bad feeling that is present in you when you are in that state... an unhelpful way of thinking... which has been caused by external events reminding you of old feelings and attitudes old pains old worries... and think about the events leading up to	Indirect suggestion

	when you started to feel bad that way...		
	in particular think about ...		
	[describe the issue or behavior that brought them here. Make sure the emotion is brought out and they are in touch with the feeling that goes with the unwanted behavior.]		
	Can you feel that feeling now?		
	[keep describing and evoking the feeling that underlies the unwanted behavior until the person confirms that they are feeling it.]		
	Hypnosis induction		
	Good... that's good... and now take a deep breath... ahhhh... and another deep breath... and one more deep breath... and just allow the whole of your body to relax... that's good		
Resources	Now that you are relaxing... you can allow your mind to change things for you... you can use the inner power that is in all of us...		Pre-supposition
	and I want you to imagine that inner power... and just for a moment allow your eyes to close.. that's right...	V	start the induction
	and as you lie there... relaxing... I wonder if you can imagine some dark dim place somewhere... some place safe and warm and comfortable...	V	pacing
	and imagine there is a speck of light... and imagine that speck of light moving... and imagine that speck of light guiding you safely down... and down... and as that speck of light moves you feel yourself drawn down and down...		guide into trance
	and thinking about that speck of light... you can feel your body slowing down... your eyes getting heavy... and the weight of your arms and legs... feel your arms and legs getting tired and heavy... imagine the whole	K	kinesthetic induction

	of your body getting heavy and tired... and relaxing... deeper and deeper now...		
Capability	imagine going deeper into that dark place... as that speck leads you on... gliding further down... imagine your body sinking... drifting... deeper and deeper...	K	kinesthetic induction
	and feel yourself relaxing... easing... sinking... like going down into the deep dark blue waters of the ocean...		
	feel yourself slowly, gently... following that speck... deeper and deeper... more and more relaxed... and imagine that speck of light is leading you through a long dim corridor... and as you go down that corridor...	V	visualization induction
	every sound you hear makes you even more relaxed... allows you to drift even deeper... and all around you... things are becoming quiet and peaceful... and every sound becomes soothing and gentle and every sound is leading you down and down as you relax those sounds right out of your mind... everything is disappearing...	A	sound induction
	and just thinking about that speck of light... imagine it now spreading soft gentle light everywhere... feel yourself wrapped in that light... cocooned... held gently safely... drifting away... supported by that light...		
	a tiny speck of light... soft and indistinct... like a quiet glow... and now imagine that glow begins to spread around... and as it does ... as it softly spreads out ... you feel yourself somehow spreading... easing... letting go...	M	metaphor induction
	feel yourself going deeper and with each passing moment...		
	the feeling comes over you that nothing really matters now... as you relax more and	K	relaxing

	more deeply... you feel that you don't really care any more... just letting everything go...	
	and as you go deeper... just imagine the tiny muscles of your eyes... becoming so relaxed... so relaxed... it's as if you just can't open those eyes... as if those eyes are glued tight shut... and you just cannot open your eyes...	Depth test
	and just feel those eyes relaxing completely... letting go... deeper and deeper... that's right... [do a depth test]	
	Hypnotic transformation	
	and relaxing even deeper... I want you to allow your mind to drift around... to drift around to the feeling you got... a feeling that things were not right and you couldn't address them... a feeling that you were [name whatever it was, repeat and expand the feeling until you are sure that the client is experiencing it.]	Beginning the Affect Bridge
	Allow yourself to get in touch with that feeling... think about the feeling... become aware of that feeling of [name the feeling]	
	and as your drift in that place now... being in that place really allows you to get in touch with those feelings... to become aware of those feelings... to allow the feeling to come up... to make itself known...	
	and now imagine taking that feeling... and going down a long dark corridor... taking the feeling with you. And as you go deeper and deeper down that corridor.. that feeling gets clearer... more defined... you begin to get an appreciation of exactly what it is...	Permission to examine the feeling
	And as you go deeper into that corridor... other things begin to become clear... other things begin to emerge... that have to do	D	Suggest resources

	with that feeling...		
	and as those things emerge... things begin to get lighter... you begin to become aware of old feelings... old ideas... things that happened... things you did... things you said... things that were done to you... things that were done to you that have to do with that feeling...		
Rules	and as you go deeper still... all those things are beginning to crowd in on you now... things you never really thought about before... things that never seemed important... things that when you look at them one way mean one thing... and then in a different way mean a different thing... and when is the right time to change the rules...		Re-examine old beliefs and rules
Capability	and as you go down that corridor... just imagine that you could take that feeling... and hold it... you can actually take that feeling in your arms...		Turn the feeling into an object
	and become aware of that feeling in a new way... and as you drift deeper and deeper... become of aware of that feeling as an object... imagine it has turned into an object... any kind of object, and notice its shape... its size... its color... the texture... think of what thing it most resembles... what it's like...	M	force attention to all aspects of the object
	notice that as you go deeper and deeper... the feeling begins to be animated... you become aware of it as a separate life... something separate from yourself...		Dissociation - you are not the feeling
	and that thing you are carrying in your arms... that feeling... you begin to think of how it might change... how you could change it... what might happen to it... how those other things in that place can be used...		begin the change

	to transform it... change it... how you could explore new forms...		
Capability	and take a moment now to experience that place and that feeling and those other things... and the secret power of transformation that lies within all of us... that inner power you have... that you can contact and use in that place...		Suggest unused resources
	that power to lift something out of yourself and allow it to transform into something else...	I	lift it out
	and still carrying with you that feeling... that feeling of [describe the feeling that is the problem]		
	and you can become curious about it... what it is for... how it got there... and as are thinking about that... the corridor begins to open up... and you find yourself in another place... and in that place there are many things... things that you could find uses for...	M	new environment = new abilities
	you can find a place... where you can set that feeling aside... and consider it objectively... and start looking for all those other parts... all the parts that make it up... all the parts that fit with it... all the parts that make you make sense of it...		
	now give yourself plenty of space as you go... and look at that feeling... examine it... become more aware of it... become aware of how it connects to all those other things...		
	and as you do... also become aware that you can become very curious about its origins... and as you do... you can open up an insight into it...		Metaphor change
	and remembering deeply now... everything that had to do with it... and perhaps there is one particular incident... one particular time		Change the object = change the

	that you felt [that problem feeling] and you weren't able to deal with [problem feeling description] and while you think of that incident, you can take that feeling... and begin to change it... begin to work with it... begin to think of how you can shape it... mold it... break it...	feeling
	and all those other things round about can become resources... things that make it possible... make it easy... and you can take that thing and transform it in many ways... and see what comes out of it... what the result is... and in that place you can keep trying new things... trying different things ... trying old things...	use the resources
	you can keep working with that feeling until at some point it will change... at some point you will go... ahhh... 'Now I understand' and then it will be like you just sweep it away... and you do that thing... you can transform it... you build trust... you have the right to do all these things...	assumption = it will change
	And so now... you can stay in that place... doing all those things... making the changes you want... turning and molding and shaping... like a workshop... and you can do whatever you want in there ... whatever is necessary... whatever you need is in there... maybe disguised... but it is there...	
	and you can work on that now... allow your mind to roam... to make those changes in your mind... and you can stay there for as long as you need... and your mind knows how to do this... and you'll know when it is done... and you might be surprised at what you leave that place with...	Give them time to make the changes
Capability	so now allow yourself to continue working	Permission

	on that thing... safe and secure.. in the knowledge that in that place nothing can harm you.. you can think about things that might have been forbidden... things that you never felt comfortable with... in that place all those things are open... all those things are possible... there are no boundaries, there are no limits...	
	other people's opinions don't count down there... only you and that feeling... and you can work on that feeling... and transform it... maybe transform it into something useful to you... something you'd enjoy... or maybe you will break it into pieces and do something with them... maybe it will just start to vanish in its own way...	Seeding ideas for change
	it will be interesting to find out... and your mind has already started on that... and so allow that process to continue... as you relax totally... to go about it in a way that feels best to you...	
	And you become aware of everything that has happened in that place... and staying deeply in that relaxed state... your body is completely relaxed... knowing that in that place... nothing can harm you...and you have the ability to step aside and look at things from a different perspective now... to choose what you want to have happen... and just let it happen...	
	Reorientation	
Capability	and when you are done you can either continue sinking into a deep blissful sleep and wake up when you decide to... or when you are done... perhaps you will just find yourself... in a happier place...	=
	and slowly counting to yourself quietly from	

	ten up to one... and when you get to one you will be back in the present... and everything will be different...	
	so take as long as need... as long as you want... to continue in that place... doing what has to be done... and choose how you want to come out..	
	so take a deep breath now... and go deeper on that journey... as if you are wrapped up in a cocoon of healing light... and nothing outside will disturb you at all... until the time is right and you decide to come back to the present.	

Self Hypnosis for weight loss

Self Hypnosis is simple and easy. This script shows you how to put yourself into trance, anywhere, anytime. Self-hypnosis can be very liberating. Many people feel a spiritual connection with something when they go into trance. Everyone's experience is unique, and it changes over time.

You can record the script and play it back to yourself, or you can study the structure and put yourself into trance by going over it in your mind. Both methods work well. Eventually, after some practice, you will be able to slip into trance just by willing it.

But you can also use self-hypnosis for personal therapy. You can use that deep connection to change things about yourself that you cannot normally access.
For weight loss people often say that they want to eat healthy food. However, the issue is seldom about how to eat healthy. Most people already know how to eat healthy. That is not the problem.
The problem is eating badly. What is needed is to focus on why you eat bad food. It is not the behavior that is important; it is what motivates you to behave that way when you know you shouldn't. So you need to focus on what it is that happens just before you eat unhealthy food.

Generally, what you need to do is to allow your mind to drift in trance and then bring up a memory of the last time you felt the urge to eat badly, even though part of you knew you shouldn't. Keep thinking about that situation. Think about the feeling that you had at the time, allow your mind to go where it wants to go, and you will get some earlier memory, or a symbol or a deep feeling from the past that you recognize. Whatever it is will represent what it is that is making you prefer to eat badly.

You will probably not get much further than that the first time you try it. But do it again, and you will find that you can begin to think questions about it: what is the purpose of this feeling?; what message am I getting about this feeling?; how could I respond?, etc.

At some point you will get an insight into what is driving your behavior. Once you understand the origin of your behavior you will be in a position to change it.

	The induction - Relax the body...		
	Take a deep breath... and let it go...		Slow down
	Now take another deep breath... and as you breathe out... just allow your whole body to relax and go limp...		the breathing
	and on the next breath... allow your eyes to close...		eye closure
	Now become aware of your body... notice if there is any tension anywhere... try shrugging your shoulders and letting them drop... tense your legs and let them relax... roll your neck and let it relax... anywhere that is not loose... just tense and relax... until your whole body feels loose and heavy... and allow that feeling to continue.	K	Physical relaxation
	First Deepener - count down		
memory	And now I want you to imagine a line... or a chain or something like that... and I want you to imagine the numbers one to ten are spaced out along that line... and I want you to make the distance between number two and number three double the distance between one and two... and the distance between three and four is twice the distance of the distance between two and three... and so on... each number is separated by twice the distance of the previous number...	V	Always offer a number of possible ways to form the line.
Capability	And just imagine going along that line... from one to two... and two to three... and three to four... and the distances between each number gets longer and longer...		
	And as you think about that line... just imagine that in your mind you are sliding	I	

	along the line... and as each number passes you get more relaxed... more at ease... and you can just feel yourself sinking ... down and down... and just keep doing that... and your breathing will get slower... and your pulse will get deeper...		
	And as each number comes along it gives you more time to relax... to let go...		
	and when you reach ten... you can just allow yourself to drift down and down some more... deeper and deeper... more and more relaxed... down and down...	>	
	allow that feeling to develop... you don't have to think... you don't have to do anything... all you have to do is to enjoy that lovely feeling of deep, deep relaxation...	I	
	and you can forget about everything... just allow your mind to drift away...	D	
	and if any day to day thoughts come into your mind... that's OK... you can just stack them off to one side... and deal with them later... they're not important... nothing is important now...	D	
	... and each breath out is taking you deeper and deeper now... more and more relaxed...	>	breathing deepener
	Second Deepener... Visualization		
	And now allow your mind to think of something you can write letters on... a blackboard or a big blue sky... whatever you want...		options
	imagine writing the letter 'A' ... and then just imagine wiping away the letter 'A'...	V	
	and then imagine the letter 'B'... and then just imagine letter 'B' being wiped away... disappearing... in any way that makes sense to you...	V	

109

	and keep on thinking of the next letter... and as you wipe away the next letter... you can feel yourself... loosening... relaxing... getting more and more comfortable... letting go...	>	disappearing = relaxing
	and as each letter disappears you can become more and more relaxed... more at ease...	>	
	And you can continue putting the letters there... and fading out... and getting more comfortable...	>	who is 'fading'?
	and you relax more and more... until it becomes too much trouble to think of the next letter...	D	amnesia
	and then you can just relax completely...	I	'when' bind
	allow your mind to drift away... to a place where there is nothing to think about... nothing to worry you... relaxed and peaceful and calm...	V	Dissociation
	Self-Test Convincer		
	and as you drift deeper and deeper... become aware that one of your fingers or perhaps a thumb will feel the need to move... and that will be a signal to tell you that you are in trance... your body can just move on its own ... without thought... just allow that to happen ... don't assist in any way... a finger or a thumb will want to move... and that will a signal that you have achieved the state of trance...	I	Give time - allow for those with a slow sub conscious
	It may be just a tiny tremor... and you may be surprised at what you experience...	K	Accept any signal
	and while you are in this state, notice everything about this state... and learn ... so you can recognize this state...		Anchor the feeling
	a state of unconscious awareness... of being in two minds... peaceful and relaxed.. and	>	Reassurance

	you can stay in this state as long as you like. And in this state many things are possible...		
	Overeating Visualization		
	Now... allow your mind to just wander...		
Memory	bring up a memory of the last time you felt the urge to eat badly, even though part of you knew you shouldn't. Keep thinking about that situation.		
Memory	Think about the feeling that you had at the time, about eating badly, allow your mind to go where it wants to go, and you will get some earlier memory, or a symbol or a deep feeling from the past that you recognize.	V	
	do not force anything... do not strive or try or do anything except accept what comes... lying there lazily thinking about times when you eat badly... when you have to eat... something takes over... something makes you eat...	K	
	an image or a memory or a feeling will form... just accept it... whatever comes is right... sometimes you will find a muscle wants to move... it can be anything... allow it to develop and observe what is going on...		Allow for all possibilities
	[If nothing comes, that's OK. You have learned how to go into trance. You should not expect to get something every time. Keep practising. Try again later.]		
	Allow the thing to just be itself... just be curious about it... Become aware of what it is doing. Be an observer. Do not try to make sense of it, do not challenge it.		
	once you have that awareness... you can begin to interact with the image or symbol or feeling or whatever comes up.		
	you will find that you can begin to think		

	questions about it :	
	Keep wondering about the thing... let it reveal itself to you...	
	Begin to ask 'will you allow me to know what this is for?' 'why is this thing here now?'; 'what are you trying to tell me?'	
	Allow an answer to form. Keep thinking different questions about it until you get something back.	
	Now think about another question... ask 'Is there some different way that I get the same effect, the same outcome... without the eating behavior?'	
	Allow your mind to weigh that idea, and accept whatever comes... Nothing in your own mind can ever harm you.	Safety
	At some point you will get an insight into what is driving your behavior, why you are doing it, and what you can do instead.	
	[Once you understand the origin of your behavior you will be in a position to change it.]	
	So take as long as you need now... and those changes can happen for you...	I
	[long pause]	
	And then, when you are ready... you can begin to return from trance...	
	The Reorientation	
	And so before coming back to full awareness...	bind
	take whatever time you need now... to consider those ideas... those images... to allow your mind to examine things from every aspect... like a jeweler looking into the heart of a diamond...	

	and the lessons and possibilities... consider them deeply... absorb them deeply... into your very being... thinking about how best to apply them...	bind: best
	And when you have had enough time to process and learn from this session... then it is time to bring this session to a close, a comfortable close...	bind: time
	and you can start coming back to the present... at whatever rate is right for you.	
	So take as long as you like to consider these things...	
	And when you are ready... you can come back to the present...refreshed and awake and alert and ready for the rest of your day.	

Bonus Scripts

Self Confidence Hypnosis Script

This Self Confidence hypnosis script reframes the client's perception: it changes the perception from fear of being judged and criticized, to having a task to perform in every social interaction. The task is to put other people at their ease, to make small talk and get them talking. By giving the client a task to do the client's focus changes from internal focus to external focus. The client doesn't have time to worry about what the other person will think, because the client is busy assessing what aspects of the other person to comment on. Because the client is forced to actually look at the other person the act of looking is a trigger for a post hypnotic suggestion to kick in, specifying that what the client will see are signals that confirm the other person's warm regard towards the client.

The script also addresses the client's core belief issues which are usually about feelings of inadequacy, a feeling of never being good enough. These are replaced indirectly by overhearing remarks that the client has actually arrived at where they are supposed to be, that the client can stop striving because the right level of performance has been achieved. Then the client is given an action metaphor for leaving behind all the things that were holding them back. Each of these metaphors can be used on their own for other types of problem. The final sections relate to common situations where confidence is needed: only one is given here. The therapist can use none, one or several of these depending on the client, and other scenarios can be added to address specific problems.

	Lead the client into trance...	
	Use your normal induction and confirm level of trance, then start the therapy section...	
	Capability: you can change	

Rule	When people like yourself **think about change**, they realize that change happens all the time, doesn't it?		Truism, Tag
	And I'd like you to take a few moments now to experience yourself a little differently...		Dissociation
	to think about possibilities... think about change.		Open ended suggestion
Capability	You know, [Client Name], people are changing all the time ... every day your body changes...you replace every cell in your body every three months...you yourself changed from a child to a teenager to an adult... automatically and without knowing how...		Truism
Capability	and that shows that change is easy and natural for you... isn't it?	D	Tag
Behavior	**...you are already changing in many ways.**	D	Lack of RI
Behavior	You can change the way you dress, you can change the way you work, you can change the words you use to talk to people, can't you?		Truism set
Capability	And therefore you can change the way you feel about yourself.	>	Sensory distortion
Identity	And this means you can easily see yourself become a different more confident person.	>	Visualization
	Capability: you can think differently		
Rule	I once met a man in Bombay [use anywhere exotic] who told me the way to get confidence is 'fake it till you make it'.		Dissociation
	Now... isn't that an interesting thing to think about?		Tag Question
Capability	And I wonder how EASILY you could imagine what it would be like to '**Fake it till you make it.**'?		Adverbial modifier
Capability	Take a moment now and imagine yourself doing that..., next week or next month		Visualization

Capability	maybe, just pretending to be confident..., confidently acting confident		Rehearsal
Capability	And for you to be confident of being confident you need to **be confident** in your ability to be confident so **you can be confident** you can fake it confidently till you make it confidently. And you might have to fake faking it till you can confidently fake faking confidence confidently until **you are confident** that you can have real confidence faking fake confidence confidently, and **you can do that**, can't you?	D	Confusion Deepener
	Henry Ford became the richest man in the world by creating and running the Ford Motor Works. He started life as a farm mechanic but became a success because he had a clear idea of how the world worked.	>	Metaphor
	He said something that I think you might want to ponder. 'In every situation', he said, 'it doesn't matter whether a man believes he can, or believes he can't, he's right'.		Paradoxical suggestion.
Rule	So you see, confidence is a matter of believing in yourself.	D	
	And I wouldn't tell you to believe in yourself ...		Misdirection
	because, you know, I think you remember how you used to believe in yourself and you know you can again.		Missing RI
Capability	There are some things you are already confident about... you are confident about your name... you are confident about how many toes you've got, aren't you?...		Truism
	Memory: you can remember successes		
Memory	And I would like you to take a moment		Reconnec-

	now... allow your mind to drift... go back into your memory... allow your mind to range over things you have done in the days and months past... and in years long ago... I want you to go back to a time when you were very confident... every day... in every thing... there was a time when you were naturally confident... and you can think back over your life... even when you weren't confident there were times when you were confident... and find times when you a acted confidently... when you did exactly the right thing... and you knew you were doing the right thing... and get that feeling again... bring that feeling up now... and really feel the confidence you had then... that feeling of confidence that you remember... and now go into your memory and identify every instance ... every time that you acted boldly... and confidently... bring all those memories... every one of them to mind ... right now...		tion
	and when you **think about it**... there are many things you already feel confident about, isn't it?	D	Grammatical inconsistency
Capability	And that means [Client-Name], when you choose to, you can feel totally self-confident about things you choose.	=	Missing RI
Identity	If you believe you can, you can.	D	Lack of RI
	You can become aware of change		
Capability	And you are sitting in that chair getting more and more comfortable with yourself knowing **you can start to feel self confident now**.	D	Ambiguity
	Every change you perceive means your confidence is rising and giving you a positive outlook.	>	

	You may already have begun to realize that you are becoming aware of the changes and I'm wondering how eagerly you're looking forward to using them?		Bind
Behavior	The old structure of your life is changing, and making way for a more solid and happier existence. In the days and weeks coming up, you will be free to explore new opportunities and new relationships.	I	Open ended suggestion
	You can learn confidence		
Behavior	Before you go into a new situation you take a moment to stop and imagine how good you will feel,	I	Visualization
Capability	and that imagining makes you feel confident because you know as you begin to feel good about yourself your confidence begins to grow.	>	
Identity	You are filled with confidence.	D	
	And I'd like you now to think about some situation you might find yourself in where you need confidence.		Rehearsal
	It could be at work, or a social situation, or something else.		Every possibility
Capability	Think about all the ways you can take control of that situation and how good that makes you feel. Imagine yourself dressed exactly right, saying the right thing, using the right gestures... fitting in with what others say, what others expect... showing you are in command of yourself, getting respect. See yourself looking good. Hear your own voice, confident, sure, convincing. Feel how you stand, how you move, how you smile..		Rehearsal
	Experience that feeling that comes with total confidence		Sensory

	How good does that make you feel? What part of that do you enjoy the most? Now I'd like you to double that feeling...and double it again.		Fraction-ation
Capability	And get used to that feeling because you have the confidence to get that feeling more and more from now on.	>	
Behavior	And always in situations like that, some little thing you see or feel, reminds you instantly that you have changed now, and you begin that process of building more confidence on your confidence, growing ever more confident.		Anchoring
	You are in control now		
Rules	You feel in control and sure of yourself in every situation. You evaluate the situation before you choose the best way to react. You always use the right words and gestures to match the expectations of the other person.	D	
Identity	You are secure and confident in every situation.	D	
Behavior	You always act confident ...	D	
Capability	...and your act is so good you convince yourself.	>	
Identity	You stand confidently, dress confidently, move confidently. Your voice is strong and steady. Your handshake is firm and friendly. You look people in the eye and you smile easily. The way you hold yourself... you communicate with your whole body... you let people know you are pleased to see them... you signal that you share their views and values... that you are a worthwhile person... that you look forward to meeting	D	

	them... You always know exactly what to say...		
Identity	Everything about you broadcasts confidence...	D	
	...and this makes others react to your inner confidence...	>	
Identity	...and their reaction confirms you are confident now.	>	
Identity	You believe in yourself. You know who you are. You like who you are. You know you are as good as anybody.	D	
	You are a winner		
	I wonder if you can imagine yourself at a gathering, a party of some sort, lots of people are talking, mingling, there are drinks and nibbles and everyone is relaxed and having a good time...		Visualization
	and you enter the room ... feeling great... looking great ... you mingle and greet people... you are dressed superbly... you look well... poised... confident... people look round and smile... ask you to come over... and you just have a quick word and move on...		
Identity	everyone admires your poise, your control, your self-confidence ... you believe in yourself... you can see it in their eyes... the friendship,... from some... respect, from others... a bit of nervousness as well... some people are unsure of themselves when you are around... you impress them with the way you walk in ... as if you own the place... you belong there...	D	Sensory
	...there are many people there... every one you know in fact... people from work... people you know socially... people you		

	hardly know at all... people you haven't seen for years... friends, family, colleagues... all there because you are there.		
Behavior	you are the star of the party... it is in your honor... to celebrate how you have changed... how you are showing automatic confidence in everything you do now... how you make everyone feel good... in your dealings with them...		
Capability	and as you talk to this one and that one... you hear snatches of conversation... *"Doesn't [client name] look so assured? I wonder how (s)he does it?"* *"(s)he's so good at what (s)he does."* ... *"everyone admires the way (s)he's changed and now takes charge."* ... *"I hear there's talk of a new job."*		
Identity	And from further back you hear *"[client name]'s the best son/daughter i could have hoped for."* ... *"I have always been proud of her/him even though i maybe never said it. And i am even more proud now."* ... *"[client name] has become everything i ever wanted her/him to be."* ... *"now, it's time for her/him to build on those achievements in her/his own way. (s)he has exceeded everything i ever dreamed of."* *"[client name] can now go her/his own way... (s)he has nothing left to prove to me."*	I	
Memory	And as you leave that party you **take with you those words you heard**... and they become a part of you... burned into your memory... something that you will never forget... at odd moments those words come back to you ... ... and each time they make you feel good about yourself...	D	Post Hypnotic Suggestion
Identity	And maybe some part of you thinks you	D	

	don't deserve those words... maybe some part of you doesn't want to believe... many people are proud of you, you know... and you can be proud of what you have achieved... after everything that has happened... **it is time for you to reassess what you think about yourself**... to really consider if you are being truthful... or if **you can now allow yourself to believe the best about yourself**... to think about all your good qualities... all you have to be proud of...		
	You can leave the past behind		
	and the feeling that you are taking something away with you is balanced by another feeling, now... because **you have accepted those words**...	>	
	you can leave some things behind as well, ... ideas, feelings, things that have been holding you back... as you leave that room you can become aware of those old things dragging behind you... like the train on a queen's/king's gown... like pulling a broken down car... and now... you turn suddenly and slash out behind you... you cut through the ties...it falls away from you ... you can leave it all behind, can't you... dump things and move on...		Metaphor
	and as you do, you feel a weight lifting off your shoulders... you breathe easier... you feel something stir within you... free to change, free to be everything you want, now.	D	Sensory
	You can be different when meeting people		
Capability	Everything you have learned today will help you to understand yourself and others better.	D	Open ended suggestion

Environment	When you believe in yourself, the more you meet new people the more you enjoy the sensation you always get	>	Sensory
Memory	and you forget about how you used to doubt yourself...		Amnesia
Perception	because you can always find a moment to remind yourself that they are really looking forward to meeting you...	>	Reframe
Expectation	...people are always curious about other people		Truism
	...aren't they?..		Tag Question
Capability	Being comfortable when meeting people is something you can learn.	D	
Rules	Some people feel that if they don't have something important or clever to say then other people will think they are stupid. The truth is that really confident people always say really simple things.	I	
Rules	Starting with really simple, unimportant things... like the weather or parking... signals to the other person that you are not a threat, that they can relax when you are around. And that's the most important step in starting a conversation: helping the other person to feel confident.	I	
Rules	The really confident person, you know, always aims to say something to put the other person at ease...	D	
Rules	... and confident people will tell you *the simplest way to put someone at ease is to get them to talk about themselves'*.	I	Indirection
	Everyone loves talking about themselves, don't they?		Truism, Tag
Memory	And when you get people talking about themselves, this means you can forget about	>	Amnesia

123

	yourself. You can forget to be nervous.		
Capability	That shift in your awareness allows you to enjoy relationships, tasks and challenges.	>	Non sequitur Open ended suggestion
Perception	And you can begin to **notice** those little gestures they use that show their interest and kindliness		Discrimination
Stimulus	and you could be surprised		
	at how much you enjoy anticipating that little feeling that comes just before you introduce yourself...		Reframing
Identity	...that tells you you are connecting with your own inner self confidence and so you are reminded every time that **you are a confident person**.	>	Sensory Distortion
Behavior	The result is you act so relaxed and comfortable around people that you could find yourself noticing and enjoying that little bit more flair and style that comes from your increased confidence.	>	
Identity	**Meeting people is something you look forward to.**	D	
	and afterwards... you go over in your mind everything you did that made it go so well and so enjoyable... and you feel good about your performance.	>	Visualization
Identity	**Meeting people makes you feel good.**		
	You have changed for ever		
Capability	As this session comes an end... in a few minutes... not now... you will find yourself feeling stronger... more powerful ... different... and with a deep feeling that something has changed... you have rediscovered your natural confidence... you remember how to be confident... you know		

	what to do in situations... you have learned to use old skills and new skills, haven't you?		
	And as you come back to present... as I count... you can allow yourself to imagine what your days will be like from now on...		Visualization
	see yourself getting up in the morning... a smile on your face... feeling good about the day ahead ... before you go out you check yourself in the mirror... that confident person smiles back knowingly... you get to work or somewhere like that... you see how you walk into the room... like you own it... you walk with poise and respect... you look smart... act smart... you greet everyone and see the respect in their eyes... you carry yourself with new self respect.		Rehearsal
	You know to them you look like a different person... and inside there is always that little feeling, the tingle you get that tells you that you have changed... that that confidence is bubbling up inside you like a secret laugh you can't suppress...		
Identity	You are relaxed and comfortable in every situation... confident and self assured.	D	'Yes' set
Capability	Because you know you have a choice, don't you?	>	Conversational Postulate
Capability	You can choose how you feel, can't you?	D	Conversational Postulate
Capability	You always feel confident now, don't you?	D	Conversational Postulate
	So now I am going to start counting from five up to one. And when I get to one you will be awake, feeling great and filled with the new feeling...		

Five...four... three... two...one...

Write your own future

A Hypnotic Metaphor Script for a journey to self discovery, self awareness and getting over the past: help your clients to forget the past, change their past hypnotically to create a different future.

This hypnotic metaphor takes you into a room full of books. Some are ancient and some are brand new. These are books of lives. Your own life is there. You take down the book and open it and inside is the story of your life. By examining the book you can rewrite the bad things in your life, with self discovery you discover the reason for what happened and then discover what your future holds.
If you have psychic abilities this hypnosis script will develop your psychic powers and make the future known to you. Everyone wants to forget the past about something.

Target	Induction section		
	Before you begin going into your hypnotic trance now just make yourself comfortable. Just settle yourself down and you can relax now. All you have to do is to focus on becoming comfortable.	D	Bind
	Take a moment now and wiggle about until you are in the right position for what comes next.	I	lack of Reference
	Look around your body and notice if there is any tightness, or any discomfort, and maybe just shrug everything until you are happily settled down and ready. If anything is making you uncomfortable then fix it.		
	Fixing things stops them bothering you doesn't it?		Truism
	Now, in a moment I am going to count down from ten to one, and when I get to one you will have relaxed into a deep satisfying trance. But before that you can move every part of your body as you become loose and		

	floppy and relaxed.	
	Now take a deep breath and relax it. Just let it all flow out... ahhhhh. That's right. Now tense up your whole body, and then let go again... really relax... and feel how good that is...	Progressive relaxation induction
	TEN... focus your attention on your feet ... think about your feet... think about letting your feet and toes and ankles relax and get loose.	
	NINE... Now relax all the muscles in your legs... in you calves, your knees your thighs... very relaxed... feel those legs getting heavy and heavier...	
	EIGHT... now feel that relaxation spreading into your body... your chest...	
	SEVEN... and now feel that relaxation in your shoulders... spreading all the way down your arms... down to your hands... your fingers... and those arms feel so heavy... so relaxed... it is as if they belong to someone else...	
	SIX... and now allow your neck to relax... and become aware of your face relaxing... your cheeks... your jaw... your lips ...	
	FIVE... let your eyes relax... your eyebrows... your forehead...	
	FOUR... and everything feels loose and heavy... as if your arms and legs were made of stone... totally relaxed... you can feel the weight pressing down... and you just can't move those arms and legs now... and you can enjoy this feeling of total relaxation... letting go... and the more you relax the more you can relax...	
	THREE... and as your mind drifts off you	

	feel a wave of relaxation travelling down your body ... down and down... from the top of your head... relaxing your face... relaxing your neck... your shoulders your body... spreading... down and down... gently and easily... feel your body sinking down... safe and warm and secure...		
	TWO... and each soft gentle breath out... is relaxing you more... and that relaxing means you can relax deeper and deeper now... letting go... drifting away... nothing matters... enjoying that that lovely feeling...		
	ONE... and totally relaxed now... totally at ease... and your mind can drift away to a place... far, far away... a place where you feel relaxed... where you feel comfortable... always... and think of what the place is like... what other places there might be that you make you feel comfortable... maybe a beach at twilight... or a favourite chair... or snuggled warm in bed on a stormy night... or maybe floating in warm water... allow your mind to drift over these things and other things... whatever feels right for you... as you drift ever deeper... enjoying the feeling ... nothing matters... nothing is important... just being in the moment... let your mind empty...		Dissociation
	Create your own future		
	And now I would like you to allow your mind to wander... wander far away... to a far distant land... a land of magic and wonder...and you find yourself walking through some trees... your feet are kicking up dead leaves... a smell of decay and renewal drifts up... as your feet uncover the rich deep soil underneath... and around you are tall trees... and above you can glimpse	D	Dissociation

	patches of dark clouds between the branches ... the forest is silent except for your own footsteps... and the sound of your breath... there is a strange feeling around... I wonder if you can feel it too? ... it's as if everything is waiting... an anticipation... of some wonderful event...	
Capability	Because you are on a mission... you have to find and enter a stronghold... a place that holds something important for you... a place you have tried to find in the past... and never succeeded up to now.	I You can succeed
Capability	But this is the day, this is the time. Now, everything can be different.	Unspecified
	You walk on... not really sure of where you are going... or what you have to do... and ground starts to rise and the going gets tougher... and just ahead there is someone struggling along dragging a bundle of firewood... you catch up... the person is old and infirm... with watery pale eyes... those eyes turn to you... and in them you see ancient wisdom... acceptance... pain... and hope.	
	And without thinking you pick up the load with one hand and with the other you start to help the old person over the hard ground... Nothing is said... you go on letting the other person lead you... until you come to a faint path in the trees... the other person shakes off your hand... gathers up the wood... and points along the path...	M Helping them = deserving to change now
	... you take that path... follow it ... and it gets wider... clearer... and the trees begin to thin out ... the sky brightens up... and up ahead you can see parts of a large building... through the trees... it has towers and high	

walls... it seems strong and enduring... but the path continues on towards the building... a private path... that goes round the side of those great walls... that takes you along the foot of the walls... walking quietly in the cool shadow there... and the path leads to a small door... set low down in the high wall... like a mouse hole in a giant's castle... and there are steps down to reach the door... you go down the steps carefully... counting them to yourself silently... and each step takes you down and down... yet with each step you feel more comfortable... more sure of yourself... more relaxed... more in charge...

And at the bottom of the steps the door swings open for you... smoothly, silently ... and inside you are inside a large room inside... it extends away on all sides as far as you can see... and everywhere are shelves... shelves filled with books, papers, journals, diaries, newspapers, report cards, evaluations, references... a vast library lies under that forbidding looking building...

you walk towards the back, going ever deeper in with each step... on each side are books on shelves, some are very ancient, their covers blackened with age, smelling musty, spines cracked and split, falling apart... and some books are only a few pages long, almost brand new, fresh and shiny, bright and youthful... and if you listen closely, you hear a murmuring... a quiet sound seemingly coming from each book... like a conversation overheard in the night... and as you pass each shelf you get a feeling... a tingle... as if the life of the author had reached out and touched you... and you realize that this is a special magical place...

each book represents a life lived... each book is the sum of living so far... a record that grows and changes...

And as you reach the central area... that same ancient figure appears again... and points off to the side... to a particular shelf... and there... one particular book is lying by itself... waiting for you... unique and special... with your name on the cover... | v

The book opens and the pages begin to turn, slowly at first... and then more quickly... and as they do... you get glimpses of pictures... smells... sounds ... tastes... people... places... voices... colors... words... all these things and more come to your mind as the book flickers through the pages... and you find you can control the pages... you can will the book to slow down... go back or go forward... or speed up... and each page is an event from your life... you can imagine it... relive it... examine it ...

And in your mind... you hear something... you know somehow that the book is offering you a choice... a chance... you can relive events... any event... or you can experience the event differently... experience the event from the viewpoint of the other people there... or an outsider's view... you can look at the event through the eyes of a stranger... understand how they would think of it... you can imagine different outcomes for the event... or all of these things... you can go back to any event as the adult you are now... and change how it happened, how it turned out... you have the opportunity now to rewrite things in your life... to have them turn out the way they should have... or to diminish the event... to make it of no

	importance... or to experience all the good things that would have come from the event if everything went your way... to grow and change as if the event had happened that way...	
	Because there is a whole section of the book... the end section... the book flips to those pages... and you see that the words and pictures are all moving, flowing, changing, ... as if the words and letters were alive... crawling across the page, slithering from line to line... and you realize that the future has not been written yet... that the future is not fixed... it depends on how you choose to experience the past... how you think about it... and you have the opportunity now to think about your past differently... and you have the opportunity to rewrite your future... you can look in the book, look at some pages from the future... imagine the future as you want it to be... and that will make it so.	
	You become aware of a presence near you... once again that old figure is by your side... and in your mind you can hear words... a voice speaks... you can choose three events in your life... any three... you can go back to those pages... and have them turn out the way you want them to... the way that would have been best for you... or can change the consequences... or any part of those events... You can let go of past hurts, failures, pain, wrongs... and by rewriting them in the book, move on... maybe you can find it in yourself to forgive... or you can look ahead, become aware of one landmark event in the future, imagine a goal is achieved, a target found, some specific event comes true in every way	

	you want it to... and you can write that new future in the book... and it will happen.	
	... break the link between things in the past and how you feel and act today... because you can choose to forget... and write your own future now.	
	And now you can go deep inside... allow your unconscious mind to identify three things in your life, things that still affect you now... or learn your goal, your destiny to come... or imagine a totally different outcome, in whatever way is best for you... and vividly experience how you want those things to be, and how you can use the choices you have now to change how those things affect you... break free of the past... break the link between things in the past and how you feel and act today... because you can choose to forget... and write your own future now.	
	So start rewriting now...	
	Reorientation	
	And take as long as you want to experience that feeling of renewal...	
	...that feeling of relief... that you are rewriting what was... not what had to be...	
	And when you are ready to move on... you can start to come back to the present... you can silently count up in your mind from five to one and when you get to one you will be back in the present and ready for the rest of your day...	
	so, when you are ready... start counting in your mind... now.	

Weight Loss Checklist

In order to replace the beliefs the client has about eating it is necessary to first identify what those beliefs are. This checklist of questions is used to remind the therapist to cover every relevant aspect of why, when and how the client eats. The aim is to identify what it was in their early life that made them feel bad about themselves. This can be dealt with by Regression and Inner Child work, by Core Transformation, NLP, Focusing, Metaphor Therapy, Cognitive Therapy or Direct Suggestion.

Weight loss therapy needs to pay special attention to the environment in which the over-eater grew up, and what was happening in their life when the problem eating pattern started. Successful weight loss therapy usually succeeds when it removes or reframes the beliefs and attitudes arising from this time.

Remember, most weight issues are actually about self-esteem. The real problem is often a core belief that they are just not good enough. Any stress today reminds them of how bad they felt growing up. Eating allowed them to feel better for a while, and they are still trying to use that cure. Fix how they feel deep inside, show them that they can handle today's stress by fixing the original source of stress, and the client will sort out the eating habits by themselves.

Using the checklist can identify resources the client already has that might be utilized for direct suggestion. These answers provide a unique set of targets and resources to use during hypnosis. It is a good idea to send the list to the client before you meet them. Tell them that they just have to read the questions; they do not have to write out answers or anything. That way they have time to think about it for a few days and this will often bring to the surface ideas and feelings they have not thought about for years.

In the office, the therapist would not normally ask all these questions directly as laid out here. Most of the information will come out naturally as the client describes their eating behavior. The check list is just to ensure that no potentially useful areas are missed.

WEIGHT LOSS CHECKLIST	
HISTORY	
When did you start being overweight?	Environment
What was going on in your life at that time?	Environment
Have you ever been able to lose weight?	Motivation
How did you lose weight then?	Motivation
How long were you at that weight?	Resource
Why did you put it back on?	Triggers & Pressures
Have you ever been bulimic?	Control issues
Have you ever been anorexic?	Control issues
CURRENT PATTERNS OF EATING	
In what situations do you eat badly?	Triggers
What sets off the eating?	Behavior
Is there a pattern to your problem eating?	Pressures
How do you know when to start eating?	Triggers
What do you think about yourself while this is going on?	Identity
What do you think about yourself afterwards?	Self Esteem
BELIEFS ABOUT EATING	
Why do you think you over eat?	Identity, Beliefs
Why don't you just stop?	Identity, Beliefs
What have you tried?	Resources
Do you think you can stop?	Beliefs
What will happen if you keep on this way?	Motivation
PAST ENVIRONMENT	
What was it like for you growing up?	Environment
What were the most significant events in your young life?	Behavior
Were you bullied at school or at home?	Identity
Did you always feel supported and loved?	Identity
Did you feel that you never really belonged?	Identity
Did you ever fantasize about being somebody else?	Identity
How do you get on with your mother now?	Relationships
How do you get on with your father now?	Relationships

MOTIVATION	
Why do you want to lose weight now?	Motivation
Do you believe you can lose the weight?	Capability
What will others think when you lose weight?	Peer pressure
What will be different when you lose weight?	Capability, Rewards
What will you be able to do when you lose weight?	Visualize benefits
What will other people say when you have lost the weight?	Visualisation of benefits
What is the one thing that might stop you?	Resource
Have you got any fears about losing weight?	Resource
SELF IMAGE	
If you don't like your body - what is stopping you from changing it?	Capability
What would have to happen for you to be able to change the way you want to?	Rules, outcomes
What do you think other people think about your body?	Rules
What do you think when you see other overweight people?	Resource
FUTURE BEHAVIOR	
What would are you going to do instead of eating in those situations?	Alternative behaviours
What will be the biggest benefit?	Motivation

All rights reserved   David Mason © 2013

CPSIA information can be obtained
at www.ICGtesting.com
Printed in the USA
LVOW13s1449080617
537415LV00026B/563/P